EARLY SORROWS

EARLY SORROWS

(*For Children and Sensitive Readers*)

Translated from the Serbian by
MICHAEL HENRY HEIM

NEW DIRECTIONS

Published by arrangement with Mme Pascale Delpech, executor of the Danilo Kiš Estate. Originally published in Yugoslavia in 1969 as *Rani jadi, za decu i osetljive,* by Nolit, Belgrade.

Publisher's Note: special thanks are due to Michael Kruger for first bringing *Early Sorrows* to the attention of New Directions

The editor gratefully acknowledges permission to reprint the last piece in this collection, "Birth Certificate (A Short Autobiography)" from HOMO POETICUS by Danilo Kiš, with an introduction by Susan Sontag, translated by Ralph Manheim, Francis Jones, and Michael Henry Heim. Introduction © 1995 by Susan Sontag. Translation copyright © 1995 by Farrar, Straus & Giroux, Inc. Reprinted by permission of Farrar, Straus & Giroux, Inc.

Design by Semadar Megged
First published as a New Directions Book in 1998
Manufactured in the United States of America.
New Directions Books are printed on acid-free paper.
Published simultaneously in Canada by Penguin Books Canada Limited.

Library of Congress Cataloging-in-Publication Data:
Kiš, Danilo, 1935–
   [Rani jadi. English]
   Early sorrows : for children and sensitive readers / Danilo Kiš ; translated from the Serbian by Michael Henry Heim.
      p.   cm.
   ISBN 0-8112-1390-0 (alk. paper)
   1. Kiš, Danilo, 1935–   —Childhood and youth. 2. Authors, Serbian—20th century—Biography. I. Heim, Michael Henry. II. Title.
PG 1419.21.I8Z474   1998
891.8'2354—dc21   98-25223
                                                        CIP

New Directions Books are published for James Laughlin
by New Directions Publishing Corporation
80 Eighth Avenue, New York 10011

CONTENTS

IN AUTUMN
WHEN THE
WINDS COME
UP

*I*n autumn when the winds come up, the leaves of the chestnut tree fall swiftly, stem first. They make a noise like a bird toppling on its beak. But the nut itself falls without the slightest wind, on its own, as stars fall, at breakneck speed. It hits the ground with a muffled scream. It is not hatched like a bird from an egg, gradually; its prickly bur, bluish-white on the inside, suddenly bursts, and out pop mischievous little half-breeds with shiny cheeks and pearly white grins. Some pods contain twins, though they are not hard to tell apart: one has a mark on its forehead, like a horse.

Its mother will always be able to recognize it by the star on its forehead.

The boy gathers the chestnuts hiding in holes in the lawn and stuffs them into his cheeks. A sticky bitter flavor fills his mouth. The boy smiles. You climb the tree, find a well-stocked branch and wait. You make sure the angel of sleep doesn't catch you. You stay there for at least three days and three nights without eating or drinking, sleeping or resting, just watching the fruit. Like when you watch the little hand on the clock. The prickles are hard now and slightly dark at the tip. If you're not careful, they'll make little holes in your finger and your nice red blood will flow. Then you'll have to suck the dirty finger you've just used to make mud or manure pies. You might get an infection. When that happens, children die. They're put in small gilded coffins and carried to the cemetery surrounded by roses. The procession is headed by a man carrying a cross, and the boy's mama and papa—and his sister, of course, if he had a sister—walk behind the coffin. His mother is all in black, and you can't see her face, but where her eyes are, the black silk is wet with tears.

A fair-skinned young lady wearing the black smock of a school uniform is sitting in the crystalline light filtering through the half lowered venetian blinds, the sun drawing tiny gold stars on the violet cologne bottles.

Here is the secret of the fragrance of violets: the young lady, who sells pictures of butterflies and wild animals, loves the fragrance of violets more than any other. She applies it liberally, all over—on her hands, her flowing red hair (though another fragrance might go better with red hair) . . .

Someone should compose a fugue for orchestra and lilacs. Take violet bottles of essential oils onto the podium of a dark hall.

Anyone who faints—quietly, without a cry—will be taken to another hall, where the childlike, health-giving fragrance of lime blossoms and camomile will be wafting.

THE CASTLE
LIT BY THE
SUN

Orange, the best-looking cow in the village, was nowhere to be found. And he had to find her no matter what, even if it meant searching all night. Mr. Molnár would never forgive him: Orange was Mr. Molnár's best cow. So he would have to look all through the woods, farther if need be. He would ask Virág to take Mr. Molnár's cows to pasture with his own and to tell him, "Orange is nowhere to be found. She's vanished into thin air." And also, "Andy asks Mr. Molnár not to be angry. He'll do everything he can to find Orange, because he knows Orange is with calf and the best cow in the village. But she's vanished into thin air." And then, "Andy said to tell Mr. Molnár not to look for him if he doesn't find Orange by tomorrow morning, because he'll be going away forever, he won't come back to the village. He hopes Mr. Molnár won't be angry." And would he tell Mrs. Sam, his mother, not to cry? "Andy is going away forever, because he lost Orange." But Virág had to be careful about how he said it or his mother might fall down dead on the spot. So maybe all he should tell her is: "Andy has lost Orange and won't come back till he finds her." Yes, that's what he'll tell Virág. And he always helped Virág when one of his cows got lost.

But what would he tell Mr. Molnár if he found Orange and didn't get her home until late, late at night, like last time? He'd tell him that Orange had been grazing with the other cows and then suddenly disappeared, vanished into thin air.

"Is that how you watch my cows?" Mr. Molnár would say. "Tell me, is that how you watch my cows? What do you do there in the woods anyway?"

"Nothing, Mr. Molnár," he'd say. "I know Orange is with calf and I never let her stray from the other cows. But this time she just vanished into thin air." That's what he'd tell him if he found her.

All at once the boy thought he heard some branches snapping in the bushes, and he stopped in his tracks, panting.

"Orange! Orange!"

He pricked up his ears and held his breath.

Somewhere in the distance he heard a shepherd's horn. He realized it was getting dark and he would soon have trouble finding his way.

"Dingo," said the boy, "where is Orange? Tell me, where is Orange?"

But the dog just stood there looking up at him.

"What are we going to do, Dingo?" the boy said.

This time he looked the dog straight in the eye while talking to him, and the dog understood. He wagged his tail, cocking his head and whimpering.

"If we don't find Orange soon, we won't go back to Mr. Molnár," he said, keeping up his conversation with the dog, who had run in front of him, still whimpering.

They followed the narrow overgrown path in the direction of the Royal Oak.

"And you'll come with me," said the boy. "Mr. Berki won't be too angry if I take you with me. He knows we belong together and I'll give you everything you need. Think what would happen if you went back without me. You'd start barking in front of the house and everyone would say, 'Looks like Andy's never coming home again.' They wouldn't say it aloud, of course, not in front of Mama or Anna. But that's what they'd think, all of them, if you went back without me."

The dog came to a halt and started sniffing.

"O Lord," said the boy, "help me to find Orange."

Dingo whimpered again and set off. The boy realized the dog had found a fresh rabbit trail or a fox's lair. He could scarcely see him through the brush.

"That's why you and me are going to run away together. Because think what would happen if you went back without me and Mama and Anna and Mr. Berki and everybody stood there frowning and asking you, 'Where's Andy, Dingo?' Mama would be able to tell from looking at you that I was dead and she'd go to pieces and Anna would tear her hair. And our cousin Mr. Berki, he would try and console them. He'd say to Mama, 'Don't be silly, for goodness sake. Really now, how does it prove that Andy's in trouble? Dingo's come home because he's hungry or because Andy told him to.' That's what Mr. Berki would say and he wouldn't be angry, because he'd know I was dead or captured by bandits or torn limb from limb by wolves or fallen under the spell of a forest spirit. But he'd make believe the thought never entered his head, because he'd feel sorry for Mama and Anna. . . But what would he really think about you, Dingo? Oh, he wouldn't say anything in front of the others, but when the two of you were alone he'd look down his nose at you. He might even spit in your muzzle for leaving me in the lurch. I'm not saying you'd do that, I'm just thinking aloud. Remember the book I read last year? *Man, Horse, Dog?* Sure you do. The one I read while we were tending the cows along the Roman Road. And then I told the story to everybody: Virág and Laci Tóth and Béla Hermann—everybody. Remember how loyal they were? Sure you do. The whole Wild West couldn't turn them against me. . . And what if a pack of wolves does attack us? You can take care of two at least. And me? How many do you think Andy and Dingo can kill all alone in the woods? Or if the bandits take us prisoner. You undo my ropes while they sleep. The rest is easy. They're asleep, so I grab one of their pistols. No, two. One for each hand. You think I don't know how to shoot? How could you? So then we take them to the police. The police will be amazed and question us long and hard. Then they'll call in Mama and Mrs. Rigó, my teacher. Mama will be very scared, because when you're called in by the police it means I've been found dead or committed some big crime. But they'll congratulate her and tell her I've caught the most dangerous, bloodthirsty gang of bandits around: they've had warrants out for their arrest for years with no luck. And then they'll give her the reward. An enormous amount. An amount so large it would take three days and three nights to count it. They'd never put that much money in the hands of a kid even if he unarms a dangerous gang of bandits. Mrs. Rigó is there so she can count the money and so they can tell her she is required by law to excuse all my absences. And next day in school she'll say, 'Andy, stand up.' And Laci and Virág will think she's going to tell me to go outside and bring back some switches so she can cane me. But instead she'll say, 'Children, Andreas Sam, a pupil in our school, has captured a dangerous gang of bandits.' And of course she'll say he was aided by his dog Dingo. And Júlia Szábó will weep bitter tears at the thought of what might have happened to me."

He spoke in a normal tone of voice. No one could hear him but the dog. It was dark in the woods by then, and the sky above the trees' high branches was a deep blue. He made his way through the bushes behind the dog, protecting his face with his hands, his bare feet treading now moss, now dead leaves, or snapping dry twigs. He spoke in a normal tone because the woods had suddenly begun to quiver with a thousand voices, and he felt that everything was irrevocably lost. He could no longer hear the shepherd's horn, and the cows had long ceased their lowing. Virág had definitely driven Mr. Molnár's herd back in and was telling him whatever came into his head, because they had not had time to come up with a story. He was definitely making it sound bad, betraying him. The way he'd betrayed him last year when he, Andy, had ridden Biscuit, and Mr. Molnár had found out and threatened to let him go. So Virág had gone and told on him, told how a group of them had been tending the cows in the Count's Woods and lit a fire and he, Andy, had told them all the story of *The Captain of the Silver Bell,* and when they'd gone to round up the cows because the sun was beginning to go down and the shepherds from Baksa and Csesztreg had gone home, Andy realized that Orange was missing. And now Mr. Molnár would definitely ask Virág when Andy had last looked at the cows. And that stupid gypsy of a Virág

would tell him that he and Béla Hermann had agreed
that Béla would look after Andy's cows—in other words,
Mr. Molnár's—along with his own, so Andy could finish
The Captain of the Silver Bell and tell them the whole
story. Yes, that's what Virág would say when Béla Hermann let on that Andy couldn't find Orange and all he'd
done was send Dingo to look for her and gone on with
the story where he'd left off, at the point where the half-
breed heroine had gone into the cabin and told the hero
Alexander she was going to poison herself out of jeal-
ousy. "In her hand she held a small white pill, and her
eyes flashed with the gleam of the Caspian Sea. . ."

"And what would we do," the boy said aloud to the
dog, whose whimpering he was following all but blindly,
"what would we do if a forest nymph cast a spell on us?
See how good it is for me to have you here? As far as I
know, neither forest nymphs nor witches have the power
to cast a spell on a dog. So as soon as we see the castle,
you stand right in back of me and watch what happens.
Don't be surprised if we see a castle any minute now.
And don't be scared. If it's a beautiful old castle, like the
Count's behind the Royal Oak, and if it's all lit up, then it
belongs to a forest nymph. I bet you think I'm going to
run away. Not on your life. Maybe the real reason she
took Orange was to make me look for her and fall into
her clutches. Anyway, I'll make believe I don't know
she's a forest nymph. I'll just say a nice, polite hello and
ask her whether she hasn't by chance seen a cow with
calf, an orange one. Then you watch, she'll just smile to

lure me on and walk off in the direction of the castle. And you know how I'll be able to tell she's a forest nymph? She'll be dressed all in white, in something like silk, only finer and easier to see through. Nymphs always wear white. I'll make believe I don't notice. I'll just thank her and go my way if I can. If I wake up, it was just a dream. But if I don't and I can't break loose, then I'll know I'm under her spell. I'll have to stay with her for a time. Don't be angry. Just go home and try and explain to Mama and Mr. Berki that I'm not dead, only under the spell of a forest nymph. I don't want them to worry. I'll stay there for a year or two. Do you realize how dangerous it is, Dingo? I may not come out of it alive. Nobody's ever escaped. Either because they're treated so well they lose all memory of their former lives or because they're treated so badly. But I'll escape. I'm smart. I don't know how yet, but I will. For Mama's sake. She'll know I'm not dead and she'll wait for me. Just don't be scared when you see the castle all lit up, okay, Dingo?"

All of a sudden it grew lighter. The woods seemed to have caught fire. The boy and the dog stopped for a moment.

"We've got your Orange for you," said Virág. "The Baksa shepherds brought her back. They recognized her."

There she stood in the middle of the clearing, pink as a cherry in the light of the setting sun.

"She's the best-looking cow in the village," said the boy. "That's how they recognized her."

He was suddenly sorry the cow had been found. Virág might still tell Mr. Molnár everything. And he, Andy, might have spent three whole years in the castle.

CHESTNUT
STREET

Excuse me, sir. Can you tell me where Chestnut
Street is? You don't know? But it's got to be here some-
where. Maybe I have the name wrong, but I know for a
fact it's a street lined with chestnut trees. What's that?
There isn't any such street? Oh, but there must be, sir.
Memories can't possibly be so misleading.

Yes, before the war. . . There was a school on the
corner and an artesian well in front of the school. I hope
you don't think I'm making it all up. I started out in that
school; I went to kindergarten there. The teacher's name

was Miss Fanny. I can show you a picture of the whole class: that's Miss Fanny, our teacher, and, yes, the boy sitting next to her is me, Andreas Sam; then my sister Anna and Freddy Fuchs, the leader of our gang. . . Yes, it all comes back to me now, sir. The street must have been called Bem Street, because I was a member of the famous Bem Boys gang led by Freddy Fuchs (also known as Beanpole), a German or *Volksdeutscher,* as they were called in those days. . . Fantastic! Without our little talk I'd never have remembered the street's name. Bem was a famous Polish general. From the forties. Does that ring a bell? Bem? Bem Street? . . . Oh, I see. How could you remember if you didn't live here before the war. Though you might at least know if there's a street lined with chestnut trees. They would bloom in spring and make the whole street smell a bit sickly, heavy, except after a rain, when the scent of the chestnut blossoms merged with the ozone and drifted all over the neighborhood.

But I have been going on, haven't I? I'll have to ask someone else who remembers it from before the war, when it was called Bem Street and lined with chestnut trees.

You don't remember, sir? You don't remember either? Well, all I can tell you is that there was a well on the corner, an artesian well, in front of the school. And a barracks nearby. On the left. Around the corner. At the other end of the street. That was as far as we children were allowed to go. There wasn't much traffic. But that was the corner where the tracks began (for the small yellow and blue trams). Oh, I forgot to tell you that just before the war they dug a zigzag kind of shelter along the right row of chestnut trees. Our gang used to meet there. Maybe that will jolt your memory: a big dugout. There were shelters everywhere, of course, but I clearly remember that our street was the only one with chestnut trees. I realize these are all details. I just want to say that I'm absolutely certain the street was lined with chestnut trees, and those trees, they're acacias, and I don't see a well anywhere, so I don't think that's possible. Maybe you've got it wrong; maybe some other street was called Bem Street: this one looks too small. But thanks anyway. I'll have to check. I'll go and knock on somebody's door and ask if this street was called Bem Street before the war. It all seems highly unlikely. I can't believe that so many chestnut trees would have vanished. There would have been at least one left. They have a long life, trees, chestnut trees; they don't just up and die.

Really, madame, I can't believe my eyes. No one seems to be able to tell me what happened to those trees, and if it hadn't been for you I'd have wondered whether I hadn't thought or dreamed them up. You know how it is with memories: you're never sure. Thank you so much, madame. Now I can look for the house I used to live in. No thank you. I prefer to be alone.

He goes up to another door—though it is not *the* door—and rings the bell. Excuse me, he says in a perfectly normal tone of voice. Is this the house of Andreas

Sam? No, no, the woman says. Can't you read? This is the house of Professor Smerdel.

Are you sure this isn't the house of Andreas Sam? He lived here before the war. I know it for a fact. You may remember his father. Eduard Sam. A man with glasses. Or his wife, Maria Sam. Tall, pretty, reserved. Or his sister, Anna Sam. Always had a ribbon in her hair. See that vegetable patch over there? That's where the bed was. You see, I remember perfectly well. This is where his mother's sewing machine was. A Singer, with a pedal.

Oh, don't worry, madame. I'm just running through my memories. Things vanish after so many years, you know. Look: an apple tree where the head of my bed was, and the sewing machine has turned into a bed of roses. And the chestnut trees, madame, they're all gone. It's because chestnut trees don't have their own memories.

✲

You heard correctly: the house is no longer there. There's an apple tree where the head of my bed was. A twisted tree full of knots, and barren. The room of my childhood has turned into a vegetable patch, and the place where my mother's Singer sewing machine once stood is a bed of roses. Next to the garden there is a new four-storied house inhabited by Professor Smerdel. The chestnut trees have been cut down. Was it the war or people or simply—time?

Here is what happened at 27 Bem Street twenty or so

years ago; here is what I wanted to cover in one lyrical leap forward: Two or three months after our departure my father entered the house at 27 Bem Street and moved out our things: two wardrobes, two beds, my mother's Singer sewing machine. . . When the last item left the house—the daybed with the singing springs—this, Mrs. Smerdel (yes, I'm still talking to you), is what happened: "When the last item left the house—the daybed with the singing springs—the house, dear Olga, fell apart like a house of cards. I don't know by what miracle I managed to. . ." (excerpt from a letter written by my father, Eduard Sam, to his sister, Olga Sam-Urfi).

Now it's a vegetable patch. Nice green leeks you have, madame.

THE GAME

The man peeking through the keyhole thinks, *That's not him; that's not Andreas*. He stands there bent over for a long time thinking, *That's not Andreas*. He stands there intransigent, immobile, even after his back starts bothering him. He is tall and the lock is almost level with his legs, but he does not move. Nor does he move when his eyes start tearing behind the lenses of his glasses and his vision blurs. A cold draft emanates from the room as from a long corridor. He does not budge. Not until a lens grazes the lock does he move his head back slightly. *I'll have to show this to Maria,* he thinks maliciously, without realizing he is thinking it or being malicious. *I'll have to show Max Ahasuerus, the feather merchant, to Maria.* He does not know why, but he needs to offend her. *And that will,* he thinks with pleasure. *I have to show her how blood finds its way underground, show her that Andreas is not her little "Fair-Haired Boy" (as she believes), but his flesh and blood, the grandson of Max the Wanderer. And that will hurt her.* He rejoiced in advance, looking forward to her secret suffering, knowing she would be incapable of arguing with his proofs even in the silence of her inner self once she had seen what he would show her, namely, her little Fair-Haired Boy, her Andreas going from picture to picture with his sales pitch as if wandering through the centuries. And that would hurt her. So he cannot tear himself from the keyhole and keeps postponing the pleasurable moment at hand: he is unwilling, unable to reach out and pluck the pleasure of torturing her. That is why he puts it off. He waits for it to ripen by itself and fall into the mud like a ripe plum. That is why he refuses to go and call Maria at once, why he keeps peeking through the keyhole despite the cold draft emanating from it as from a long corridor, from a distance beyond time. There at the other end of the corridor in a distant, fuzzy perspective, in a crepuscular light—there stands Max Ahasuerus, feather merchant, deftly vaunting his wares, good Jew that he is. The man thinks only of him, must think only of him, because he sees him there. But he does not forget for an instant that he must show it all to Maria and that it will hurt her. The only reason he does not call her at once is that he is waiting for the moment to ripen by itself and fall like a plum so he can crush it, squash it with his foot.

✲

The boy (in the meantime) is alone in the room. He feels his hands going numb with cold and has been meaning to run and warm them in the kitchen, but he can't quite bring himself to do it. No one can see him here, while there in the kitchen with the grown-ups watching he can't play the way he does here. Maybe they wouldn't bother him and they certainly wouldn't scold him (not Mama at least) because the game he is playing is so harmless (not like lighting matches in a drawer or spitting at people in the street). Though it is a funny game. Anna never would have come up with it. He is walking around the room with a chintz pillow from the bed on his shoulder, bent under its supposed weight, moving from picture to picture (he senses there is something bad about that) and mumbling. His toys—tin soldiers, clay and glass marbles—lie forgotten under the sewing machine, at the window, on the freshly scrubbed floor. And for now he is playing another game, though he does not know its name. "Would you like some white swan feathers, madame?" he whispers, bowing, though keeping an eye on the Mona Lisa's mysterious smile above Anna's bed. His face is the picture of disappointment. This was his last chance. All the customers have said no. The old man (with a funny hat and a long pipe under his harelip) hanging over his father's bed, the distinguished-looking old woman (with a hooked nose and funny, pointy, buckle-up shoes)—all of them, one after the other—and now this pretty woman smiling so mysteriously, so ambiguously: first you think that she'll buy the lot, then that she'll turn it all down with mild contempt. The boy stands before her, hurt and—smitten. He awaits her response, thinking, This is no job for me. I'd give this woman all my goods for her beautiful eyes and her smile and my business would go under. Well, let it, he thinks, his eyes shining gently. Let it. I'm going to give her everything so she can sleep in a nice soft bed. "Madame Mona Lisa," he says aloud, "here is a gift for your bed from a young merchant . . . You have paid for it with your smile." He bows and blushes for real, though he knows it is all just in play, just a game. He is ashamed of his callow gallantry and self-deception because even if you are only playing at business you should try to sell your wares at the highest price and not go bankrupt for a smile.

✳

The man peeks through the keyhole. He sees his late father, Max Ahasuerus. It is not a ghost; it is Max Ahasuerus, goose-feather merchant, in person. He has come from afar. The man says nothing. He feels his eyes cloud over. A stiff draft emanates from the keyhole as from a corridor. *"Wünschen Sie feine Gänsefedern, gnädige Frau?"*

Max says with an impish bow, unloading the pack from his back.

The man does not respond.

"I have the finest feathers in the region," says Max to Mona Lisa. "These come from Leda's swan. Can I interest you in pure swan feathers?" Then, seeing the smile on the customer's face, a sad smile combining contempt and compassion yet promising little, he hoists his pack onto his back, bows again, and says, *"Adiós, señora.* You'll be sorry."

The man gives a start. His hands, which till then were crossed behind his back, suddenly start saying something the woman cannot see because she has turned away. Even then Eduard cannot take his eye away from the keyhole. But all at once he stands up and wipes his eyes with his handkerchief without taking off his glasses.

"Maria," he says softly, "guess who's in the bedroom? Here, have a look. But be careful."

The woman turns without letting go of the Turkish coffeepot licked by the burner's purple flame. "Who, Eduard, who?" She can see the pupils narrowing behind his glasses.

"Who? Who? See for yourself!" he cries angrily. "My late father. Max Ahasuerus!"

He collapses wearily into a chair and lights a cigarette. She takes the pot from the fire. Her hands are trembling visibly.

✳

The door creaks and the boy gives a start. The woman finds him with a pillow in his arms. There is no one in the room but him.

"Andy," she says, unable to control the flutter in her voice. "What are you doing here in this freezing room? Your hands must be numb."

"Nothing," he said. "Playing."

"Put that pillow down this instant," she said.

"But the pillow's part of the game, Mama," the boy says, placing the pillow on his shoulders and planting himself in front of her. "Can I interest you in some nice swan feathers?" he says with a smile and a bow.

The woman does not respond. The smile disappears from the boy's face (yes, he knew it, he sensed it, there was something bad about the game). She tears the pillow out of his hand and flings it onto the bed. Then she heads for the door, but stops, rooted to the spot by the man's look. She lets go of the boy's hand and walks quickly past him.

"Did you see Max Ahasuerus?" he asks her. The question falls like a ripe plum in the mud.

"Yes, Eduard. Yes, I did. He offered me swan feathers. 'Can I interest you in pure swan feathers?'"

✳

"Once upon a time there was a king," the woman starts in after the evening prayer.

"And?" the boy asks, brushing the sleep from his eyes (though he knows that as always her story will put him to sleep and that his efforts are in vain).

"And the king married a Gypsy girl."

"Why?"

"She was beautiful. The fairest in all the land. And one day she bore him a son, a son to inherit his kingdom. And the king, happy to have an heir, ordered the Gypsy girl killed, because if word got out that she was the boy's mother, the boy would lose the throne. So he never knew who his mother was. Luckily he looked like his father, and no one could tell from the color of his skin that he had Gypsy blood in him."

"I don't understand," says the boy.

"It doesn't matter," his mother says, somewhat regretting having begun in that vein, but unable to stop—and not only because of the boy. "Just listen to what happens next. . . The boy was brought up by the wisest of wise men in the kingdom, and the king was happy as could be."

She might well have stopped there, because she herself had no idea how to end it: it would be hard on the boy. But when she heard the boy's "And then?" (he was already good at finding the right word), she went on before having come up with an ending.

"One day the king looked into the boy's room to make sure the prince was asleep."

"And then?"

She hesitated for a moment, but went on.

"And he found the child holding a velvet and silk pillow and standing in front of a picture of his mother, begging (she put on a Gypsy accent at this point): 'A crust of bread, all-powerful queen,' he heard him say, 'and a rag to cover my nakedness. . .' The king rushed into the room, beside himself, and grabbed his son. 'What are you doing, prince?' he cried. 'Begging, Father,' said the prince. 'I'm tired of my toys and horses and falcons, and I'm playing beggar.' She spoke more and more softly until finally she was silent. The boy had fallen asleep. She turned out the lamp and started to leave on tiptoe.

"Did he kill his son too?" she heard in the dark and jumped. She turned and caressed the child. "No," she said in a whisper, without turning on the light. "He didn't."

THE POGROM

The desire not to miss an event that involved virtually all the street celebrities I knew, as well as my secret intention to untangle the net of events intruding on my life at the time, gave me the courage to join the crowd of people rushing past. Panting strenuously, trying to match my breath to their steps, I was carried along shoulder to shoulder with tax inspectors and firemen. I hoped thus to capture the sense of events that had profoundly shaken me and that not even my mother had been able to explain. On I went, struggling with my fear.

The snow crunched beneath our feet, we packed it
down, it grew hard as a slab, brittle and resonant, we
trampled it like a gigantic caterpillar, a pure, white steam
rising out of its mouth. Through the screen of fetid
evaporations and exhalations and despite the filter pro-
vided by the snow, I could distinguish the smell of cheap
cologne and sour sweat permeating the green uniforms
of the tax inspectors and the blue uniforms of the firemen. Suddenly I heard a crash of broken glass and saw it
flash like lightning above the crowd. Then, like a distant
echo, the cracking of boards and, finally, the door having
yielded to the pressure, a long sigh of relief.

I stood my ground outside the entrance to the warehouse, clinging to men's coats, women's skirts, pressed in
this direction and pushed in that, but always returning
through the forest of legs, borne on by fear, convinced
that here in the heart of the danger I was safer from
these people, knowing that I must not withdraw from
the shelter of their rage, that I must not retreat one inch
from their tentacular mass or they would grab me and
trample me underfoot.

Since the warehouse door opened out and no one up
in front would move back, there was no way to get inside, and a terrible fracas broke out, with people shouting and waving sticks in the air, stamping their feet and
crying for help. Then suddenly, by what miracle I cannot
tell, the large door sliced its way into the dark mass like
the blade of a knife. A bluish dusk had begun to fall, an
enormous elevator traveling down the steep walls of its

cage. The air reeked of petroleum and soap, and the warehouse's open maw now spewed layers of the most varied scents, prefiguring the oranges and lemons, the toilet soaps and spices inside. Then out flew a barrage of canned food—the tin clinking cheaply, the innocuous table-knife sheen lighting up the dark—of candles bundled together in blue wrapping paper and rattling like dry bones, of apples falling with a thud only to be ground underfoot as if chewed. Sugar gushed out of brown paper bags, it too crunching underfoot and mixing with the slush. People hugging bundles of loot in their arms like children had trouble extricating themselves from the crowd. The flour floating in the air like face powder and coating their eyebrows gave them a festive if somewhat clownish look. One woman was biting into a bolt of silk she had pulled out from under her coat. In the flash of a match that lit up her face I glimpsed her teeth, pink from the silk's reflection. I watched a roll of flowered chintz wind stubbornly around people's legs and heads like crêpe paper streamers on New Year's Eve. It started getting tight, and some women screamed, which only provoked the milling crowd, and people took to pushing and shoving and tugging furiously at the material, while it kept welling forth out of somewhere like a river. When there was nothing left in the warehouse but bare walls and darkness, people quickly dispersed, clutching their booty under their coats.

I was standing off to the side by then, like a righteous man spared retaliation. A good-hearted woman took

notice of me and stuck a can in my hands. It had a color-
ful label with SPAGHETTI ALLA MILANESE in big red
letters on it. I stood there for a while holding the can and
not knowing what to do with it, lacking the courage
either to throw it away or to take it home. I kept looking
over at Mr. Anton, the tax inspector, who was perched on
a barrel tossing fistfuls of confetti into the air.

A STORY THAT WILL MAKE YOU BLUSH

A night at sea near the coral reefs. I check the pistol under my pillow. Perfect. If there's a mutiny on board or Joe Mammoth's men show up, I'm all ready. All I have to do is open the porthole. It's a tropical night, sultry. I can hear the gulls calling. I need a good night's sleep. I've got a hard day ahead of me.

"Hey, Andy! How'd you do with the homework?"

"Don't know. Came out all right, I guess."

"What a dumb topic. What's there to say? What did you write about?"

"Mama going to Baksa. I'm waiting for her down by the river, and I get these cramps like a hungry wolf. Then she comes back. That's all. I describe the smile of the bread in her basket."

"You come up with the strangest things! 'The smile of the bread in her basket.' What's that supposed to mean?"

"I don't know. The way it smells maybe. What did you write about?"

"The way my mother bakes bread. The way she goes up to the attic and brings down the flour, you know, and puts the loaves in the oven and then takes them out. You know. What everybody wrote. You're the only one who writes that la-di-da kind of thing."

"Know what? I need to pee real bad, but I'm too lazy to get up. It's so nice here in the shade I can't bring my-self to go all the way to the lavatory."

"Funny, me too. I was just about to pee my pants. But there you go, all la-di-da again. Lavatory! Toilet's the word and I can think of worse words too."

"The bell's going to ring soon and we're going to wet our pants. At least I am."

"Then turn the other way and do it here. I'll cover you."

"I thought of that, but what if a girl came along. I don't think I could get it going."

"Of course not. You're too la-di-da. Oh, well. Take my hand and try to get up. I'm not helping you because I'm your only friend in the school but because I've got to go real bad myself. And if the bell rings, we've had it. . ."

"Hey, Andy, you piss like a horse. It's like you've been at it for an hour now."

"Has the bell rung?"

"Not yet. There must be something wrong. Maybe Mrs. Rigó had something important to attend to. Or it has rung and we didn't hear it."

"Where's everybody else? Do you see them? Can you hear anybody?"

"I can't tell. I think they've gone in. Gosh, Sam, aren't you ever going to stop? Shut it off, will you. Turn the spigot. When I'm going at it and somebody comes along, I make believe I'm looking for something in the grass and when they're gone I open up the spigot again and finish off. Doesn't that ever happen to you? You're pissing away and a girl comes along. Or Mrs. Rigó or somebody."

"Look, you go ahead. I can't go back to class till I've emptied my bladder, and that's all there is to it."

"Can't you even try to stop?"

"You go ahead. The flood's dying down, I think, but I've still got some left. . . There, now I feel better. . ."

And suddenly I'm horribly aware that I'M DREAMING THIS. I'M DREAMING THIS and I feel a warm liquid inundating my thighs. Oh no, what's Mama going to say! And—even worse—Anna! I'll never hear the end of it. She may even tell somebody. I'd better check and see how wet I am. Maybe it hasn't got to the sheet yet. Then

I'm saved. I'll pull my trousers on over the wet under-
pants and they'll dry out in school.

I turn over on my side and feel the sheet with my hand.
Horrors! I'm lying in an enormous puddle that's spread-
ing. How many times have I sworn this wasn't going to
happen again. I usually manage to wake up at the last
minute. But not always. And now I've gone and done it.
I ought to be ashamed of myself, really. Why couldn't I
see what was happening? It's crazy. Peeing for a whole
hour in the school yard. A two-year-old would have
known it was a dream. It must have been that damn tea I
kept drinking yesterday.

I lean over and whisper into Mama's ear, softly, so
Anna won't hear.

"I wet the bed, Mama."

It takes her some time to wake up, and she doesn't
understand me at first.

"I dreamed I was in the lavatory at school and I wet
the bed."

Slowly, still half-asleep, she feels the sheet under me
and smiles when she gets to the puddle. She picks the
clock up from the bedside table and presses it against her
ear to check if it has stopped.

"Better go and change," she whispers to me conspira-
torily. "It's time to get ready for school."

Then she gets out of bed—carefully, so as not to
wake up Anna—opens the wardrobe, and gives me a
change of underwear. A dirty autumn dawn, humid and

sullen, enters our room. The thought of rising, rain, and school is devastating. The sudden awakening and the mocking, vengeful shame of my dream makes things even worse. I go into the kitchen with Mother. She pours out some water from the pot for me to wipe my eyes and nose with. I feel better now. I've managed to ford the dirty, tepid river between sleep and life. My body is infused with a kind of animal warmth, and I can picture myself running barefoot to school, going into the classroom all wet and frozen and taking a seat near the stove, silent, full of myself from the pity provoked by my bare feet and wet rags. Later, when I'm dry and back in my own seat (my feet are out of sight and the red of my hands is gone—I might be wearing white gloves), my best pupil halo will return and I'll perch there wearing my crown, wise as an owl, while Mrs. Rigó reads out the best composition (mine) in an exalted, sing-song voice, after which silence will reign until Mrs. Rigó recovers from her agitation and announces her intention to have the composition published in *The Good Pastor* for its edifying and inspirational character.

SERENADE FOR ANNA

I heard some noise under the window and thought they'd come to kill my father.

But then a violin called everything into question and calmed my fears. The person playing the violin under our window was no virtuoso, but he was clearly taken with my sister Anna. The violin had an all but human voice. Someone head over heels in love with the stars and my sister was singing shyly, but trying to make his voice sound as deep and virile as possible. It came out like a whisper:

Why did the Lord create love?
Why are the nights. . .

Anna finally found some matches, and in the flash of the flame I saw her standing at the curtain all in white. And when she went back to bed, I heard my mother say to her, moved, yet in an almost sententious tone of voice, "Remember, Anna. You must always light a match when you're serenaded. To show you've heard."

Comforted by my mother's voice, I sank back into sleep and a forest of fragrances, a green meadow.

On the ledge the next morning, we found the branch of an apple tree in bloom, looking like a silver crown, and two or three flaming red roses. And long before our teacher could ask (that day in school), "Who is the brute who trampled my roses last night?" I had recognized the flowers from Mrs. Rigó's garden by their scent, because I was the one who tied up her rose bushes and trimmed her lilacs.

I didn't want to say that, judging by his voice, the brute browsing in her roses was Mr. Fuchs, Jr., the shoemaker, my sister Anna's secret admirer.

Tell me, Anna, did I make it all up?

(The flowers and fragrances.)

THE MEADOW, IN AUTUMN

The circus artists have gone, the strong men and the bear trainers. Autumn is on the wane. Here in the Little Field or the Count's Nook, as people still called it, the packed down dirt and trampled grass constituted the principal remains of their stay—that and a hole a meter deep in the middle of the meadow, plainly visible among the flattened molehills. This is where they planted the main pole of the circus tent, thick and rough-hewn at the base, fine and slender at the top, with a flag flying from it. The earth around the hole is completely bare, the clay from down below easily distinguishable. It is not the hole from the year before or the year before that, as might be thought. Because circuses come and go, small provincial circuses made up of Gypsies and magicians, tightrope walkers and strong men—every year, in autumn, like a final summer festival, a pagan celebration of sorts. Though it is never the same troop or the same tent or the same hole. Last year's hole had disappeared and no one could say where it had been: it had closed up like a wound, but even better, because it left no scar, covered as it was by earth, grass, and weeds. This year's would disappear as well, eroded by rain and filled in with earth. Then the snow would hide it for a time, and when the warm spring showers came they would bury it under earth and grass as if it had never existed. And that would be the end of the autumn festival that had flourished under the pink big top.

Good-bye fair, good-bye tightrope, good-bye sniggering monkeys and trumpeting, lumbering elephants. The circus left as suddenly as it came. Early one morning before sunrise some muscular young men in sailors' shirts, whose feats had made people gasp for days, pulled out the stakes, took down the wires and ropes, and toppled the pink tent and proud, flag-topped pole. Then they packed it all skillfully in their wooden, ship-like caravans, and off they went, quietly, as if sneaking away, the wheels of the caravans creaking mournfully, and through the open curtains at the windows you could see the magic fish-women bustling about making breakfast, the blue smoke rising out of the chimneys barely visible against the morning blue of the sky. The animals roared in their cages; only the elephant tagged along at the end of the procession, dignified and lethargic, fanning himself with his ears.

Now, a mere day or two after the circus's departure, the traces of what had gone on there are still fresh. All over that broad area, broader than the circle inscribed by the tent (you could make out its borders by how firmly the soil was packed), there are sparkling beer bottle caps finely fluted around the edge like flowers, sodden cigarette butts, half-eaten apples, rust-colored fruit pits, crushed ice-cream cones, footprints of horses and people, dried circus-animal droppings, bread crusts, the old newspapers spectators had sat on, children's drawings torn out of notebooks, empty cigarette boxes, match boxes, torn paper bags crawling with ants. On the spot where the old shaggy pony had stood the earth is flat and devoid of grass, though a few wisps of crushed straw trampled black do remain. Farther on there are traces of the monkey tent, a square with rough-hewn oak stakes at each corner, still shiny on top from the flat of the ax that drove them in. Although only a couple of days have passed since the departure, the grass has started coming up again here and there, springs of green metal bouncing back miraculously, in a delayed-action operation, as if foot or hoof had just gone.

Outside this firmly packed field the grass is thick, fragrant, dotted with late-blooming wild flowers, blue and yellow, and all manner of weeds, which spring up triumphantly, stifling with their tentacles—already rust-colored at the tip but nonetheless vigorous therefor—the tender stems of flowers and blue-green grass. This is the last spurt of growth for the grass, the last surge for the roots. The plantains are heavy with seeds, the leaves of the weeds have begun to darken and wrinkle, turning along the edges into claws that scratch at one another. There is a battle going on here, but one invisible to the eye—the weeds triumphantly raising their sabers and long tentacles out of the luxuriant growth; the flowers, caught by the voracious weeds' insatiable invasion, making a last-ditch attempt to grow, emitting quite excessive fragrances. Intoxicated, enthralled by the heavy scents and deceptive jumble of colors, bees and insects buzz frenetically through the redolent battlefield, clashing with blowflies and wasps, with butterflies and bumblebees. An occasional grasshopper, bloated and heavy, the color of dying leaves, will fly noisily across the meadow only to fall, listless and unwieldy, in the dense tangle of vegetation like a piece of ripe, wild fruit.

Such is the meadow, the bare autumn meadow, after the fair.

Suddenly my father emerges from the grass on the west side, brandishing his cane. He stops at the edge of the packed field where the monkey tent stood and leans over, training his rigorous, knowledgeable eye on autumn's disastrous effect on the flowers. It lingers on a piece of crumpled paper sticking up from the grass, standing out from the exuberant autumn green in its deathly pallor. First he grazes it with the tip of his cane, as a bird will graze an unknown fruit with its beak; then he bends, smoothes it out and, near-sighted as he is, sounds out the Gothic letters. It is a recipe torn from a German cookbook, one the circus artists and strong men doubtless used to maintain the elasticity of their limbs and firmness of their muscles: sorrel sauce. He shakes his head, angry and disdainful: he obviously does not approve of the German recipe, whose absurdity in these days of war is tragically plain. He has his own, proven recipe for sorrel sauce using no fat, only salt and water, though of course requiring an admixture of aromatic herbs and spices widely available but whose names he keeps secret. That is why he frowns, why he goes on reading with an ironic smile on his lips. Then, carried away by the text, which only reinforces his belief in the superiority of his way, he turns it over, heedless of the crust of human excrement running diagonally across the Gothic letters. "So that's your sour cream!" he cried jubilantly. "That's your Gothic gravy!" He straightens up, pleased at his bit of vengeance, and with a precise fencer's lunge runs through the page with his cane so he can keep it for a while as a reminder. Then he steps back into the tall grass, clutching his herbarium (*Herbarium Pannoniensis*), in which a variety of dried herbs and wild flowers lie pressed between the pages like rare stamps: daisies, Saint-John's-wort, sage, saffron, *Gypsophila peniculata. . .*

ENGAGED TO BE MARRIED

It was before his father started drinking (or rather the period between the Two Great Sprees, as his mother later put it) and before he, Andreas Sam, started working with the peasants. So it was the second or third year of the war and the boy was no more than eight or nine. He was sitting in the cart, drunk on the odor of freshly mown hay and gazing at the sun going down over the horizon, bright red.

"Good day, Mr. Sam," said a peasant, lifting his greasy hat. So it must have been before Mr. Sam—his father, in other words—started drinking.

His father lifted his stiff-brimmed hat.

"Good evening. See? The sun's going down."

"It'll be windy tomorrow," said the peasant. "Red after sunset, wind on the morrow."

"Right," said his father, resuming his place behind the slowly moving cart.

The child didn't know whether his father had noticed him. The scent of the dried clover made him giddy and listless. He suddenly began to shiver and huddled into the hay. His father and Mr. Hermann were talking about him. "He's turned into a real little scamp," he heard his father say. That referred to him, he knew, but he didn't say anything; he just burrowed deeper into the hay, the intoxicating scent of clover and camomile having all but knocked him out.

"Let me tell you, sir," said the peasant, "he'll be running after the girls before long."

"Before long!" his father said. "Why, he did something the other day I'd be ashamed to tell you."

Hearing those words, the boy realized his father knew about *that*. But what pained him more was that his mother had betrayed him: she had promised to keep it a secret. If it didn't happen again.

"Well, let me tell you, sir. . . ," the peasant went on, but the boy put his hands over his ears so as not to hear what they said. His head was spinning from the dried camomile—and shame.

This is what happened, the terrible thing that makes

him blush even now. (Let us stick to the third person. After so many years Andreas may not even be me.)

They were playing hide-and-seek in Mr. Szabó's courtyard. Mr. Szabó is Júlia's father. It was Saturday, after school. Farkas was it, and while he counted they ran and hid in couples: Otto and Marika, Erzsike (Júlia's sister) and Oskar, Júlia and Andy. He had long been taken with Júlia. They were in the same class and they were the best pupils—he among the boys, she among the girls. She had better penmanship than he had and was quicker with her answers; he drew better and wrote better compositions.

Andy went to the Szabós' often, because his mother knitted sweaters out of angora wool for Mrs. Szabó and her daughter. He went more often in winter to borrow food. He would stand at the door and say, "Praised be Jesus and Mary," and then, "Mama asks Mrs. Szabó—if she has any and if it isn't too much of a burden—whether she could lend us a loaf of bread. Stale bread is fine. Mama thanks her for anything she has and says she'll work off everything she owes by summertime." He would take the bread wrapped in a linen napkin and thank her (again) and run home to make his mother happy. But he never lingered in Mr. Szabó's house.

"I'm going to write you a letter," he whispered.

They were lying on a pile of hay in the barn. They could hear Farkas's hoarse voice coming from outside: "Fifty-five, fifty-six, fifty-seven, fifty-eight. . ."

"I know what you're going to write," she said.

"No, you don't," he said.

"Yes, I do."

They had to stop talking. They could hear the barn door creak.

"There's somebody in the hay in there," said Farkas.

They knew he couldn't see them. There was a long silence. They knew Farkas was still there, straining his ears. Then they heard his footsteps on the gravel moving away from the barn. He hadn't closed the door.

"No, you don't," he repeated.

"Yes, I do," she said.

"I'll give it to you tomorrow in school. I'll put it in the catechism. Page thirteen."

"Why page thirteen?"

"Because," he said.

"All right," she said, "but I know what's going to be in it."

"Swear you won't tell."

"All right," she said, "but I know what's going to be in it."

"No, you don't," he said. "And when you've read it, I want you to burn it and blow away the ashes."

"Why?" she asked.

"Because," he said. "So nobody else can read it."

"They've all been found by now," she said.

"You go first," he said, "and tell them you were in the stable."

She slid down the hay and ran off. He didn't follow until he heard her ringing laugh down in the courtyard.

He was it the next time, but later they found themselves back in the same spot as if by agreement.

"I know what'll be in the letter," she said. She had braids the color of hay, a turned-up, freckled nose, and a large mouth. She smelt of dried clover.

"How about now?" he said. He could scarcely speak. "Do you want it now?"

"I'm scared," she said.

"Me too," he said.

"Swear you won't tell."

"I swear," he said.

"I'm scared," she repeated.

They lay very close to each other. She closed her eyes. He kissed her. She had a dimple in her cheek and a little turned-up nose covered with freckles. She smelled of clover.

"I'm scared," she said.

"Me too," he said.

Once they were there for a long time and Farkas found them.

"Andy and Júlia are man and wife," he said.

"It's not true," said Andy.

"Man and wife," Farkas repeated. "They're always together."

"There's nothing between us," Júlia cried.

"Then why are you blushing?" Farkas asked. "Why are you blushing if there's nothing between you?"

Júlia burst into tears, which gave the game away, and from then on things went downhill. Andy was stronger than Farkas, so he smacked him. Farkas ran away and complained to Anna, Andy's sister. So Andy decided not to go home for dinner. Or the next morning for breakfast. Or ever again. In summer he'd catch fish in the river, and in winter he'd go from village to village helping peasants. And when he'd saved enough money, he'd buy a boat and go to his grandfather's in Cetinje. Or anywhere. He'd become a gangster or a detective. It didn't matter.

He hid along the river bank until dark, but then it got cold and he started shivering. From the cold and out of fear. He was sure that Anna and his mother were looking for him all over the village. His mother might even die of grief if he didn't go home before dark. So he decided to put off his trip and set out for the village. As he got close, he heard Anna calling him. He called back.

"Come home," Anna said, but she didn't dare go up to the thicket where he was hiding, because he had a stone in his hand. "Come out. I won't tell Mama."

"Won't tell her what?" he said.

"That you're engaged to Júlia."

"You can tell her I'm never coming home again," he said with a lump in his throat.

"She'll cry," Anna said.

"Have you said anything yet?" he asked.

"Not a word," said Anna. "Not a word. I swear."

"If you don't, I promise not to go to San Francisco. Or Montenegro."

"I won't," Anna said.

Then his mother came along calling for him, and Andreas wiped his eyes, took a deep breath, and left his hiding place, whsipering to Anna, "All right then. Just remember: not a word."

But his mother could always tell when he'd been crying.

"Why have you been crying, son?" his mother asked.

"I haven't been crying," he said, heaving the kind of sigh that comes after a good cry.

And then he burst into tears. He'd just thought how hard it would have been on his mother if he'd run away.

Anna tried to help by saying, "He wanted to run away to San Francisco. Or Montenegro and live with Grandpa."

Now he had to admit he'd been crying. And to say why. Of course not for anything in the world would he have said that he and Júlia were engaged and they'd fallen asleep together in the hay. All he said was what could be said: that he'd hidden in the barn with Júlia and Farkas had found them and teased him and he'd gone and smacked him one. That was it. If they'd put him on the wheel or lit matches under his fingernails, he wouldn't have said any more.

He had been certain his mother believed him and Anna hadn't told her about the rest, about being engaged and all that.

And now he realized that his mother knew everything and had even told his father, because otherwise why would his father have said that he (Andy) had done something the other day he was so ashamed of he couldn't even talk about it?

That was why he had put his hands over his ears and shut his eyes. That was why he thought he was going to die of shame and grief. The intoxicating scent of the recently dried clover had all but knocked him out.

When he opened his eyes, he saw his father, tall in his stiff black hat, cane in hand, trailing behind the cart against the purple horizon.

THE MEADOW

He was walking along the river bank in the direction of Baksa. The air was redolent with the smell of ozone and overripe elder. The fresh molehills were red as scabs. Suddenly the sun came out. Buttercups lit up the grass. The scent of camomile rose from a field heavy with an abundance of scents. He watched his dog nibbling at primroses, green mucus dripping down its muzzle. Then he lay down on his stomach next to a molehill steaming like a hot biscuit and chewed on a still-moist leaf of sorrel.

He was barefoot and wearing dark-blue linen shorts. There were scab-covered pustules between his fingers.

(It never occurred to me then that I would one day be a writer, but I had the following thought: "When it comes to flowers, God I'm helpless!")

He was clutching two million in his pocket. Two million in blue banknotes, war banknotes. It was meant to buy him sulfur bars.

In front of the doctor's house there was a large Saint Bernard tugging at its chain. It had gorged itself on meat.

(I knew I was going to have to lie: two million was worth nothing.)

"What can I do for you, young man?" the doctor asked.

He was wearing a white smock that smelled of mint drops.

"Scabies," he said. "The itch."

(It can't go on forever, I thought to myself. Half an hour with the doctor, say, plus half an hour for the walk back. That means the whole nasty business will be over in an hour at most. In an hour, even thirty minutes, I'll be back down at the river, and the lying, the sham, the shame will be done with. I'll have put it all behind me, like the Saint Bernard's tail. It will be over and done with. I had never before differentiated between past and future. That day at the doctor's I learned that when things are bad you have to think about what is going to happen next. Like the meadow on the way back.)

The doctor wrote a prescription out of habit, then changed his mind and tore it up. He handed the boy two sulfur bars wrapped in cellophane. The boy swallowed hard and returned from the meadow, which he had started to cross in his mind.

"How much do I owe you, sir?"

"How much have you got?" the doctor asked.

"Two million, sir," said the boy.

(He was on his way across the meadow again, slicing buttercup heads off with his stick. The doctor's house and the dog and everything that went with them were all behind him now. He couldn't have gone back to them even if he'd wanted to; he could only have spun around them like a dog chasing its tail.)

"And what can you buy for two million, young man?"

"I don't know, sir."

(He knew perfectly well. An egg. At most.)

"Nothing," said the doctor.

(He was getting close to home by then. He was on the log bridge watching the water flow past, like time.)

So there he was, walking along the river bank, approaching the village. The returning conqueror. In one pocket he clutched two million in blue war banknotes, in the other two sulfur bars wrapped in cellophane.

He could just picture it: his sister Anna and his mother standing at the door, and Anna bleeding between her fingers.

He would toss the sulfur bars on the table and say, "Mix with lard. Spread on the wounds before bed."

He would forget for a second (on purpose), then re-member, and toss the money on the table and say, "He wouldn't take it. It's not worth anything. He knew."

But before that he'd stop at the log bridge and watch the water flow past.

He pictured his mother beating the sulfur in a tin bowl. Like egg yolks. It looked good enough to eat.

He was walking home along the river bank. He had conquered time. Though when it came to flowers and the meadow he was still helpless.

THE CATS

In the lilacs behind the house the boy found four blind kittens. Even though their whining told him they had been separated from their mother—who was surely searching for them at the other end of the village, wailing from roof to roof—he hoped to find another cat to adopt them, an old maid cat or a kittenless cat or a just plain good-hearted cat.

If the truth be known, the boy had gone into the garden to steal currants. He was lying on his back under the bush, pulling back the leaves until the red berries hung over his head like earrings. They were spattered with droplets of mud: it had rained during the night. The currant bush was just next to the lilac bush.

The kittens, though unable to see the boy, sensed a giant tom approaching. They did not know he had come to steal currants and was at the same time scouting for birds. They squealed like infants.

The boy ran into the house and put some milk and bread in a bowl, then dipped the kittens' tiny muzzles into the bowl one by one. They merely peeped defenselessly and squeezed their gummy eyes further shut.

It was early evening.

Early next morning, before he left to drive Mr. Molnár's cows to pasture—very early, in other words— he went into the garden behind the house to see what had happened to his kittens, whether they had been adopted during the night by an old maid cat or a kittenless cat or a just plain good-hearted cat. He found them shivering in the dew with no other sign of life, the bowl still next to them, untouched. The only thing different was the bread: it had swollen up from the milk.

"There's no justice in this world," the boy said to himself. "Among people or cats."

He saw a large stone nearby. He picked it up and let it fall. One of the kittens squeaked like a rubber toy, its head caught under the stone. Its tiny paws stretched and clenched, and a red fan appeared between its nails. When he picked up the stone, he saw the kitten's head speckled with blood and one golden-green eye protruding from a split eyelid. The boy groaned and raised the stone again.

It took him an hour to do them all in.

(Although he was still red and shaking when he got to Mr. Molnár's—he might have just vomited—Mr. Molnár did not say anything.)

He waited until evening to bury them. He buried them next to the lilac bush, the stone along with the kittens. He left no trace.

GETTING
DELOUSED

"Remain after class, Andy," says Mrs. Rigó, his teacher. And since she says only "Andy" and not "Andreas Sam," it means he will have to clean out her chicken coop again. It is three or four months since he last did it.

So while everyone else makes a racket with the benches on their way out, Andy stays in his seat, wondering guiltily about how he can get Mrs. Rigó to give him something to eat when he's through. He'll need to have a good wash first. Clean under his nails with a stick and rinse his mouth out. And that makes him think about what comes before: dried chicken droppings landing on his tongue, sliding down into his lungs; dust sticking his nostrils together.

He sweeps and scrubs on his knees. When he can no longer hold his breath, he removes two tiles from the roof and sticks his head through. The disheveled head on its long, skinny neck rising above the chicken coop looks like a wild mushroom. His saliva is thick and as dark as the fresh droppings.

He puts the tiles back and crawls out feet first. When his foot touches the first rung of the ladder, he lifts the old basin with both hands. It is badly chipped—almost devoid of enamel—and filled to the brim with ash-colored chicken droppings. He leans the small worn-out broom against the corner of the privy at the far end of the courtyard and empties the basin into the rose garden.

It is autumn, and the roses are beginning to shed. A few white petals have fallen among the dead leaves, but one rose, scarlet red, is blazing like the sun at sunset. Its fragrance reaches the boy's nostrils. Bending to take a deep breath, he grazes it with his nose and it falls apart, filling the air with the aroma of dried paprika.

Now he washes in the wooden trough beside the wood shed. At first the water is so clear he can see the white clouds in it; when he bends over he can see his own face. The bottom of the trough is lined with dark green velvet.

He plunges his head into the trough.

Now there are chicken lice floating on the surface.

His mouth still tastes of badly plucked chicken thighs.

Now he knocks (he doesn't think of knocking; he knocks) on the glass door. Attila—Mrs. Rigó's son, a boy his age—lets him in. Andy walks across the rug in his bare feet. The rug is as velvety as the bottom of the trough. He is served supper in the kitchen. The table is covered with a piece of checkered oilcloth that smells of burnt milk. He is given dried cracklings on a plate and some red apples and an orange in a white porcelain bowl.

Hungry as he is, he can't eat: people are watching him. He keeps turning a greasy bit of meat in his mouth and moving his legs under the table. He can't see it, but he knows his feet will leave a wet spot on the floor when he goes. He'll be sorry tomorrow when he's hungry.

He shuts his eyes. The orange looks like the rose.

He stands and thanks Mrs. Rigó.

Mrs. Rigó puts the cracklings he hasn't eaten into a paper cone. She gives him an apple too. Embarrassed, he slips it under his shirt.

He shuts his eyes. The orange looks like the sun going down.

Later, at home, he crawls into bed on his stomach, naked, with only his head sticking out from under the comforter. His mother and his sister Anna pick the lice out of his hair and the seams of his shirt. And while his mother goes through his hair, popping the lice between her fingers, he sinks so swiftly into sleep he might be fainting. For some reason he feels like crying, but is too weak even for that. All he can do is breathe in the smell of the house and the pillow. And then he sees the red rose that fell apart in the rose garden. It gleams in his consciousness with such force that for an instant, squeezing his eyes shut at its overpowering brilliance, he can smell its aroma, the aroma of paprika.

Those are the last things he can make out: the sudden aroma and the brilliance. That scarlet blaze.

Then he sinks swiftly into a serene sleep.

Though somewhere off in the distance, in the rose garden, he can still hear the voice of his sister Anna saying, "Look where it's gone to, the nasty thing! Under his arm! Thought I wouldn't find it!"

A MUSHROOM STORY

"Simple," said the boy. "Nobody's looked here yet."

"My goodness!" Mrs. Sam cried, delighted, and emptied her sack of pine cones into the grass.

They were in a clearing at the edge of the Count's Woods, the sun bathing the dry leaves and pine needles in a red glow, the air redolent with resin and rotting hay.

"Nobody's looked here yet," the boy repeated.

But no one moved. They just stood there, dumbfounded. There were mushrooms everywhere, all along the rim of the clearing. Large ones, dark and shiny on top like loaves of bread.

"They weren't here when we passed by before," Anna said.

"True," said Mrs. Sam sententiously. "The boletus can grow to maturity in several hours, especially after a rain."

"It rained while we were at the Royal Oak," said the boy.

"True," said Mrs. Sam. "There was some lightning to the west of us. There must have been a shower here."

"I think the ground is still wet," said Anna, poking some dead leaves with her foot.

And still no one moved to harvest them. They just stood and stared. The mushrooms seemed to be growing before their eyes. They could almost see them boring up like strange worms out of the depths, through the layer of leaves, their smooth caps like mounds of dough darkening and rising.

At first they picked them carefully, sinking their fingers into the layer of moist leaves hiding the roots. Then, suddenly—because they realized that someone might come along—they started grabbing them, breaking them off, and sticking them in the sack they had emptied of pine cones. They had been roaming the woods all autumn gathering pine cones to burn during the winter and had only occasionally come upon a mushroom or two.

"Mr. Molnár gets up at three," said the boy, "and

walks a long distance. All the way to Keszthely, I think. Mushrooms usually grow in the heart of the woods."

"Now don't go blabbing to anyone," Anna chided.

"Right," said Mrs. Sam. "We found them just behind the Royal Oak. That's what we'll tell people."

"Mr. Molnár has a special place he goes," said the boy, "and he won't tell anybody."

"I bet someone'll find this place," said Anna. "It's right off the road. One cow strays and that's it."

"I'll have to ask Mr. Szabó how to dry them," said Mrs. Sam. "Then we can stock up for the winter."

"All you do is slice them along the stem," said the boy, "and lay them out on a white sheet. Mrs. Molnár dries them on the roof."

"On the roof?" Anna asked, skeptical.

"The chicken coop roof," said the boy. "First she spreads out the sheet, then she lays the sliced mushrooms on it. When the sun goes down, she takes them in, and that's it."

They didn't pick the smallest ones; they left them there to grow.

"Not a word to anyone, you hear?" Mrs. Sam reminded them. "If people ask, we found them at the Royal Oak."

"Well, I won't tell," said Anna.

"All some people need is to see a mushroom and they know where it's from," said the boy. "One look and they know everything."

"You know why he says that?" said Anna. "So he can

brag to Mr. Molnár and his new friend the Gypsy, Virág."

"I do wonder what he sees in that Virág," said Mrs. Sam.

They took a shortcut across the wet meadows. A bank of pink clouds was rising in the west beyond the village. They watched the clouds, walking silently through the wet grass. First Mrs. Sam carried the sack, then Anna helped her. Andy walked in front, digging up fresh molehills with the end of his stick.

"Evening, Mrs. Sam," said old man Horvát. "Put in a good day's work, I see."

"Evening, Mr. Horvát," said Mrs. Sam, shifting the sack to the other shoulder.

A mushroom rolled over to the old man's feet. He stabbed it with his cane.

"Tell me," he said, "what are you planning to do with those poisonous mushrooms?"

"Poisonous?" the boy asked.

"Take my advice, Mrs. Sam," said the peasant. "Toss the whole lot of them. And not in my field. No, in the river. Past the village. . . Heavens! to think if it wasn't for me, there'd be nobody left in that fine, upstanding family! Nobody but the crazy father, that is."

Mrs. Sam put the sack on the ground and was about to say something, but thought the better of it. Instead, she gave her children a tug and started off with them in the direction of the river.

PEARS

A peasant climbs a tree and shakes the branches; a number of pears plop to the ground. The ripe ones burst, and their dark, fig-colored insides come pouring out. Wasps, drunk with delight, swarm round. Peasant women smelling of sour sweat pound them with their sunburnt hands, seeking out the less ripe, more succulent ones.

The boy, who has spent all morning gleaning and binding cobs, lifts the pears to his nose and bites into them or flings them as far as he can to keep the wasps away.

"Well, well," says Mrs. Molnár, the wife of the boy's new employer, "little Andy Sam is sorting pears, God forgive me, like a dog, with his nose. We'll have to take him hunting with us. We're short on dogs. . ."

THE HORSES

The boy lay on his back on a wooden chest, staring at the smoke billowing across the ceiling. Through it he could occasionally make out the greasy black beams dripping their thick, shiny soot. Tongues of fire puffed by the wind out of the tin-plated stove hovered for an instant along the stovepipe like a horse's mane. The oil lamp burning a combination of petroleum and grease penetrated the blanket of smoke with its sputter. The wet clay reeked of horse urine. (Several years earlier the room had been used to house horses.) Even though the floor had been dug up and covered with new clay as yellow as wax, the odor remained. Humidity climbed the earthen walls, eating away at them like acid.

It was snowing, and the wind flung handfuls of needle-like crystals against the window and under the door. The pine cones in the stove hissed like saliva on burning lips.

"How come you don't choke to death?" asked the soldier, rubbing his eyes blinded by the smoke.

"We're used to it," said the boy. "Spread your blanket down here. It's warmer. And there's less smoke."

The soldier, a reservist with a prominent mustache, spread his blanket out next to the boy and began to patch up his sopping wet saddle. The boy lay next to him on the hard wooden chest. Though wrapped in his father's old coat, he was shivering. His eyes were closed, and he followed what was going on around him with his gun-dog nose in a feverish half-sleep. The sour smell of horse urine, the fresh-dough smell of wet earth, the rancid smell of petroleum, the puffs of fresh resin from the woods. And now the stable smell brought in by the soldier. (He was one of the grooms being quartered with them.)

Suddenly he heard someone stamping the snow from his shoes at the door. It was another groom. The man thrust his head through the half-open door and shouted, "Sultan's fallen!" as if announcing the end of the Ottoman Empire.

The boy jumped to his feet. The soldier stuck his

crooked needle into the saddle and rushed out. The boy ran after him.

The flame of the oil lamp fluttered about the stable like a frightened owl.

Sultan was lying on his side, motionless, in a thin layer of sawdust. His eyes were deep purple. Their stars were gone. Only the silver crescent on his forehead still shone.

"Sultan!" the soldier cried, pounding him on the rump. "Hold on, Sultan! Hold on!"

But the horse just lay there, stiff, like a toppled monument.

Then the other soldier, the older one, said, "Tomorrow the major's going to give it to us. You tell him there's no hay, and he says, 'Steal it then or grow it or dream it up!' Grow it, dream it up! But how? How, damn it! 'I know you have orders not to steal,' he says, 'but you get those horses hay if it kills you.' And now this. He'll never understand!"

He gave the horse a kick in the ribs. The head moved slightly, but nothing more.

"She's next," said the younger soldier, kicking Odalisque in the rump with his boot. The mare tottered on her thin legs, but did not crumple.

"He'll never understand," said the soldier with the mustache, " 'Grow it, dream it up!' "

"We'd better prop them with something," said the younger soldier. "We can't let the major find them like this."

They ran and got some ropes and threw them over the beam above the mare. They pulled one rope behind the front legs around the stomach and another back at the rump. Then they tightened the ropes. The boy held the oil lamp for them, shielding the flame with his frozen fingers.

To deal with the Sultan monument they had to call in soldiers quartered nearby. Again they threw ropes over the beams, but after they had pulled them under his stomach, they began shouting "Hoo! Hoo! Hoo!" in unison, and the horse slowly rose to its feet, stiff and green as bronze.

Next morning the boy ran to the stable. (It had in fact been a stable once, but his aunt used it as a shed to store shavings for her large stove.) The stable was cold; fog was leaking in at the ceiling. The horses hovered above the earth like monuments on a winter morning. Odalisque's head hung down to the ground, and her nose swayed slightly in the wind, making the same line over and over in the sawdust; Sultan's head was wedged between two high bars above the manger near a sheaf of wet hay, his crescent now extinct and barely visible in the darkness.

Soon the major arrived, panting and red with anger and cold. The grooms stood at attention, up to their knees in snow and puffy-faced from lack of sleep. The major threatened them with court martial and had a clerk draw up a statement with the particulars dictated by a civilian veterinary surgeon. Then he left with his orderly, swearing. The soldiers went into the stable without a word and took down the ropes. Odalisque crumpled into the thin layer of sawdust. Then, like insurgents, they toppled Sultan's monument.

"Go on," said the soldier with the mustache. "Kick the bucket. I knew you would."

The nag's stomach collapsed with a bronze-like clang.

The soldiers loaded the carcasses onto a sleigh and took them to the horse cemetery. The sleigh was drawn by a horse that would clearly end up there too before long, and was followed by a boy sick at heart, Andy by name, and a dog whose name was Dingo.

THE MAN WHO CAME FROM AFAR

For three days and three nights soldiers filed past our house. Can you imagine how many soldiers it makes when they file past your house for three days and three nights non stop! They came on foot and in carts, on horseback and in trucks. Three days and three nights. And all that time I watched them from my hiding place in the lilac bush. The last soldier passed on the afternoon of the third day, having fallen far behind the others. He had a bandage around his head and a parrot on his shoulder. Not until he was gone did I come out into the street. You would never have known that soldiers had been filing past for three days. Except by the silence maybe.

I was a little sorry that there would be no more soldiers coming through the village. When soldiers file past your house for three days and three nights, you start getting used to them, and then life seems empty without them: no one prancing on horseback, no one playing the harmonica.

Suddenly I saw a cart emerge from a cloud of dust at the far end of the village, and I thought more soldiers were on the way. But it was only a single funny little cart. It was pulled by what I thought were two hinnies but were actually—as I later learned—mules. The dust had so altered their color that they looked more like mice than mules or hinnies. Two mice just out of a sack of flour.

Since at that hour there was no one else in the village standing and gawking at every chance passerby, the man in the cart came up to me. He said something to me in a foreign language, so I didn't quite understand what he meant. All I knew was that when a man and a woman come from a long way off in a funny little cart they must need water. So I said, "I bet you come from a long way off."

I knew they would understand me. My father once told me that two people speaking different languages can understand each other if they are people of good will and reasonable intelligence. All you have to do is speak

slowly and distinctly and, of course, steer clear of compli-
cated matters. That's why I asked slowly and distinctly
whether they'd come from a long way off. I also pointed
far into the distance, in the direction they'd come from,
by which I meant to illustrate what I was trying to say.

The man climbed down from his cart and said, "All
you need to know, young man, is that we come from afar
and that we are in a hurry. Can you tell us where we can
water our mules?"

"I thought they were hinnies," I said, "though they
look more like mice. As for water, you will find some in
our courtyard."

The man grabbed one of the mules by the ear and
guided the cart into our courtyard. Meanwhile I ran inside to tell my mother we'd be having a visit from a man
who'd come from afar and who spoke in a strange way
but we could understand him even though he was a for-
eigner. Then I got a bucket and fetched some water from
the well. Our cousins hadn't come back from the camp
yet, and I was in charge of the courtyard and the stable,
so I told the man to unharness his mules.

While he was washing (his wife stayed in the cart), I
asked him if he hadn't met my father on his travels. Because when you come from afar, you always meet a lot of
people along the way. I told him that my father was tall
and slightly stooped and wore a stiff black hat. "They
took him away two or three years ago," I said, "and
we've had no news from him since."

The man told me that he had indeed met a lot of

people, because when you come from afar you always meet a lot of people. "And some did have black hats and canes," he said, "so your father must have been one of them."

"He walked a little funny," I said, "because he had flat feet." And I asked him whether any of the people he'd met—any of the people with black hats and canes, that is—had a strange way of walking.

"It may be," said the man, "that one of the men I met was in fact flat-footed. When one travels for months on end, one cannot fail to meet someone with a strange walk."

"The day he left the house," I said, "he was wearing a frock coat and dark trousers with white stripes. He parted his hair in the middle and wore one of those detachable collars. Have you by any chance met a man answering to that description on your travels?"

"Oh yes," said the man, laughing. (He must have thought I was a liar or a clown.) "I did once meet a man answering to that description. He wore a black stiff-brimmed hat and metal-rimmed glasses and carried a cane and all that. He had rather a strange walk and sported a frock coat, dark trousers with white stripes, and a shirt with a detachable collar. I saw him exactly four years ago in Bucharest, my boy," the man said. "He was the Japanese Minister of Heavy Industry!"

PAGES FROM A VELVET ALBUM

Darkness had descended abruptly on the woods. Mother had a premonition, a vague feeling, and she took us by the hand and rushed us home. We took turns dragging the sack of pine cones, not wishing to lose our rich harvest, our sad autumn harvest. Mother was not wrong. As we approached the village, we saw a light in our cousins' house, a ghost-like will-o'-the-wisp shining through the windows. We shuddered. Would Mother be happy to see him? Had her kind heart forgiven him? Of course it had. Because when we entered the courtyard—

not without a certain superstitious dread—and knocked on Aunt Rebecca's door, Mother shrank back. She clearly expected us to find our father and his entire family there, reconciled at last by the common sufferings and calvary of their tribe. But the only one we found was Aunt Rebecca, and the way she looked did not bode well. We were so astonished we couldn't say a word. Good Lord, how she'd changed! There was almost nothing left of her luxuriant hair: the black chignon had fallen, the curls along her temples looked scorched, as if set aflame. She stood there holding a heavy seven-branched candelabrum with only one candle burning in it. The candelabrum with the single candle was clearly meant to show us—by its missing flames, its empty branches—what Aunt Rebecca was about to announce, shaking her withered head slowly, portentously, and with great dignity first to the left, then to the right, and then once more, even more slowly: He is no more. Was it relief we felt or mute despair? My father—dead! In any case, I refused to believe in his death. I was convinced that Aunt Rebecca was not telling the truth. Oh, her face and gestures were tragic enough, but the whole thing struck me as a hoax—Aunt Rebecca's desire to get rid of my father as painlessly as possible, with a slow shake of the head. Standing so close (she had grown near-sighted) that the flame almost touched our cheeks, she shook her head again for each of us, each time with a different, meaningful expression: for Mother something approaching true compassion; for Anna a lesson (watch yourself, dear

niece); and for me a secret gloating (your belief in his im-
mortality will soon be toppled, you little smarty-pants—
time will take care of that). After a significant wink—
her mouth frozen, but her eyes crafty, smiling—she held
the flame of the candle up to my cheek, staring me in the
eye and moving her large nose back and forth. Was there
any further meaning in her pantomime? What else
might have been behind the demented luster of those
large, black eyes? I couldn't help thinking that her mal-
ice came from a desire to communicate the fact that my
father had not died a hero with immortal words on his
lips, words of wisdom, which posterity would remember
and cite as an example of his philosophical outlook and
judicious composure in the face of a horrible death, that
far from such a position vis-à-vis his executioners he
had. . . Oh, I'm sure it's true. He must have sensed the
significance of the vicious game they'd embroiled him
in, and when they put him on the left with the women
and children, the ill and unfit for labor (and he was all
these at once: a great malingerer, a hysterical woman, a
woman with an eternal huge tumor-like false pregnancy,
a child too, a big baby of his time and tribe, and unfit for
labor, any labor, mental as well as physical, because the
trajectory of his genius and industry would inevitably
veer dangerously back to its point of departure, to ab-
solute zero, to its total negation), on the left of God and
of life, he thought for a moment—if only for a moment—that he had fooled them (there was his sense of
humor, his ability to cope in difficult situations), but he

must have realized immediately thereafter, in his innards and his crazy head, that he now stood on the side of death, stupidly, of his own accord, that *they* had fooled *him,* fooled him like a child. . . . Aunt Rebecca's spiteful eyes hinted at the bitter, tragic truth: walking in the column of poor, weak souls, among panic-stricken women and terrified children, plodding along with them, alongside them, tall and bent, without his glasses, without his cane—they had been taken from him—dazed, shuffling in the column of victims like a shepherd amidst his flock, like a rabbi with his congregation, like a teacher surrounded by his pupils. . . No, not that. They beat him with their clubs and the butts of their rifles; he moaned and fell; the women buoyed him up, raised him off the ground, while he—alas!—crying like a baby, spread the awful stench of his traitorous intestines.

2

The only other member of my family to return was my Uncle Andre, he too burned by a strange fire, an infernal light that gave his skin a sick, fusty hue, the fatal stamp of a black sun. He brought home songs of the times, sad camp ballads and rabbinical lamentations that he chanted to himself out of tune or played on the ocarina, like an owl hooting.

A day or two after his return he started digging a hole in the stable where the army horses had been. Aunt Rebecca protested in vain. The soil he dug up was moist and smelled of horse urine. Before long his head disappeared in the well he had made, and the curt orders he gave to Aunt Rebecca seemed to come from the grave. To my great surprise I soon saw Aunt Rebecca hauling a bolt of cloth from that stinking hole, a bolt of chintz, all red and blue roses. She lay the catch at her feet, and what a catch it was: roses caught in a chintz net all aglitter like deep-sea fish. When she sighted the first roses—still minute, mere buds, a sparse school of blue small fry that had lain in the mesh of the net so long that they stank— my aunt started tugging nervously, feverishly at the material. But alas! The huge bolt, buried there on the eve of the war, wrapped in oilcloth and placed in a wooden box, had been totally permeated by the horses' acid urine.

Aunt Rebecca spent the following day trying to salvage what she could. She spread her huge net over the fence in five layers, counting on the beneficent effect of the sun. Overnight a hedge of climbing roses grew up around the house as around castles of old, but the courtyard reeked of urine. And in vain. She had merely brought out into the open the disastrous influence of time and darkness, earth and the amber streams the cavalry horses had sent at an angle into the earth throughout the war years like sunbeams. With tears in her eyes Aunt Rebecca did what she could to save her only wealth, her hidden treasure: she took a pair of scissors and cut up the cloth into small, barely arm-length strips, but in the end, when they disintegrated in her fingers like a spider's web, she was forced to concede defeat. All that night—to keep the peasants from seeing—she and Uncle Andre tossed rotten roses on the manure pile with pitchforks. Oh, how many terrible curses fell on the backs of the cavalry horses, how many anathemas, how many brilliant, blood-curdling similes!

3

Probably under my father's influence, the fatal traps of which she had resisted as long as he was alive, my mother took it into her head to build herself a knitting machine out of boards and old umbrellas. Although she had honed her handiwork to perfection in terms of both speed and artistry, having turned her production of needles out of bicycle spokes into a veritable little factory capable of supplying the entire district, she now wished to expand her purview to include knitting machines and supply not only the district but the entire region as well. She hoped it would release my sister and me from the fields, as she put it, and restore our civic dignity. Unfortunately she abandoned the idea with a heavy heart and at an early stage: she was unable to find old umbrellas. And so she went back to her nocturnal handiwork, by the light of an oil lamp that still burned the war-time mixture of grease, petroleum, and shoe polish, and brandishing needles with a platinum-like sheen. Those two needles. . . I say two needles, though to be accurate, I should say that her fingers played an equal role in the process—not merely as projections of her hand and executors of her will but as an integral part of her knitting kit. I have in mind primarily her outstretched index fingers, which the needles (of her own manufacture) served only to extend. Without realizing it, Mother had created her own knitting machine: a narrow canal had dug itself into the tender pulp of each index finger as if the thread flowing through it were the harsh, metal string of an instrument. That set of active needles, that magical script wove long, white, fairy-tale pages of angora wool, and when you blew on the downy surface to smooth it out a bit you would see wondrous patterns like those on oriental rugs. The secret of her magic art was simple: she never repeated anything. If a village missus ordered the same sweater as a village miss, Mother would accept the commission without attempting to sway the vanity of the local beauties, but would make a variation on the given theme, similar to it in appearance only; in fact, she would alter the script, the motifs, styling it entirely anew, so that it resembled the previous one only insofar as it revealed the hand of the master, her personal, inimitable imprint. She did so for perfectly practical reasons: only products that were one of a kind, that not even she could imitate, would uphold the prestige of the firm. Her business flourished, but not for long. The village women and war widows, prompted by her example and their sincere admiration (which, of course, as is wont to happen, soon turned into envy and slander), began themselves to knit during the long winter evenings, ineptly at first, but then with ever greater skill, and their scripts came to resemble hers—perfect imitations of the original, yet imitations all the same. Still, the copies were clever enough to deceive the uninitiated, to keep them from perceiving the poverty of the counterfeits, lacking as they were in true inspiration and spontaneity. At first Mother tried to oppose the onslaught of imitations by altering her script, by giving her art an unattractive virtuosity, but it did not work. Her skill—acquired through long, sleepless nights, through toil and moil, through inspired stitching and unstitching—made its way from house to house, shamelessly mimicked. Seeing that the charlatans were capable of imitating the master's virtuosity, she resorted to simplicity, a bareness of style, though never forgetting to slip something cryptic into her moss stitch, a mystical rose of inspiration, a mark of the master. It did not work. Counterfeit roses began appearing in the same place as hers and, though artificial, they again deceived the uninitiated. (Yet all they would have had to do was look at the reverse side of Mother's knitting, and the symmetrical negative imprint of her work—the fine knots and tracery, the minute roots of the knit—would have told them how much labor had gone into turning those broken threads, those bits and pieces into the finished picture, where the tricks of the trade were invisible and everything was clean and neat and seemed made of a single thread, done with a single stroke.) In the end, after much travail and many sleepless nights, Mother gave it up entirely and went back to gleaning in the fields: she had lost all her customers.

4

We get on the train with our ludicrous luggage, dragging behind us the tent of our wanderings, the sad legacy of my childhood. Our inevitable suitcase—terribly frayed, its clasps forever ready to open with a rusty flintlock pop—has survived the flood, floating empty on the waves like a coffin. Now, like an urn filled with ashes, it contains the sole and pitiful remains of my father: his papers and photographs. It contains his baptism certificate, his diploma, and those unbelievable torahs covered with the calligraphy of a distant, all but mystic past, the invaluable testimony of a dead poet, the archives of his grief, transcripts of court cases, documents from a Subotica brush factory (that went bankrupt on account of him), injunctions, work permits, a letter promoting him to the post of station master, and two of his own letters— his "Great" and "Small" Testaments—and his release from the Kovin asylum. . .

What induced me to smuggle that strange archive into our suitcase unbeknownst to Mother? Doubtless the premature realization that it would be the sole legacy of my childhood, the sole material proof that I ever existed and that my father ever existed. Because without all that, without those manuscripts and those pictures, I would certainly believe that none of it had ever happened, that I had made it up after the fact as a means of consolation. My father's face would have been erased from my memory like so many other faces, and if I held out my hand I would grasp at a void. I would think it had been a dream.

I hid this family archive (which I had put together just before our departure according to my own valid—as I now see—criteria) in the suitcase, along with select schoolbooks and notebooks. Of the notebooks I chose only two: the ones with my compositions; of the books I included a young person's Bible, a *Shorter Catechism,* a children's garden manual, *Mein zweites deutsches Buch* by Luise Haugseth Lamács, and *The Pilgrimage of Children's Hearts* compiled by Dr. Carolus Gigler, *censor diocesanus,* on the basis of a hymnal. I also included one of my favorite novels from the cheap popular series *Captain of the Silver Bell,* and most important, the jewel in the crown, *The Yugoslav and International Bus, Ship, Rail, and Air Guide* for 1938 of which my father was editor-in-chief (and which would take on a new life, undergo an amazing metamorphosis, its Assumption, in one of my books). I placed the *Guide* among my own things, *my* books, as a precious heirloom.

5

Among the rare documents of my childhood there is a booklet that is green as a leaf and not much larger, though by now it has turned yellow like a leaf as well. Besides the two metal staples in the crease along the middle page there was one more that went all the way through the slender volume. I put it there myself, by hand, after making a hole in each of the pages with one of Mother's knitting needles, because I had torn a page out and caused, to my great distress, its counterpart to come loose and then come out altogether. I believed I had made a fatal error by following Mother's advice and listing in that official document the reason for my absence as something that I found less than convincing, an illness—whooping cough or measles or some such thing—while I preferred the naked, humiliating truth (a preference I have maintained—in literature, at least—to the present day). After an excerpt from the school's strict regulations, which in the most decorous of terms urges teachers and parents to work together and respect one another ("We request our esteemed parents to welcome their children's teachers into their homes"), the booklet ends with a warning that the pupil is required to keep it clean until the end of the school year (whence my dismay over the loose page) and to show all comments on the day entered "to the persons concerned." The final page had a space for signatures. Under Mother's Name: Mrs. Eduard Sam, Widow. Under Father's Name—a long wavy line, empty space. That line (along with my mother's name) was written in by my sister Anna. It followed the printed line until the end, where it rose and broke off. In that single restless, jagged curve with its mild waves and neurasthenic break we may read my father's life line: his tottery walk, his fall, his death rattle; it is a frenzied cardiogram, his heart's script.

6

What else does the booklet speak of, its blank columns filled with invisible ink by the boy's imagination? It merely poses simple questions about how the pupil spends his time, about his schedule, in school and out. What is he studying? Who are his teachers? When are his classes? What languages does he speak? Here, in these question marks, in these questions without answers we find bitter regret, the seeds of a nostalgia for knowledge, of a child's secret dreams and ambitions. In these schematic questions (piano? violin?) we find the hint of a world inaccessible and unknown to me. Out of this booklet and its milky glass-door columns come the well-bred faces of tutors and governesses, of brightly lit salons and peaceful afternoons, when a doorbell rings and a pale young woman with an ethereal *Bonjour* on her lips enters the nursery to help with lessons (from four to six), bringing with her the aura of a world still in code but a code whose key she bears under her tongue like a medallion and whose meaning comes gradually to light. Shortly thereafter (why not dream a little?) the bell rings again, but more fully and richly, because this time it is the piano teacher. And soon he is flexing his long white fingers, and études pour through the nursery's closed blinds. And then? Then comes the violin teacher. A woman this time: a woman's slender figure better suits the noble contours of the violin, and she has no double chin when she lowers her melancholy head to the instrument. (No, I don't miss any of this now. It was actually finer and more useful—a word I write with trepidation—to wade barefoot through warm cow manure on cold autumn afternoons.) My sense of truth and belief in the nobility of suffering compels me to enter in the Reason for Absence column for 13 February 1944: lack of shoes. And for 5, 14, and 24 February: blizzard. . .

7

But why did we drag along those featherbeds, those clumsy bundles wrapped in brown paper and wound round with string? Why did we drag them along when Mother had no trouble leaving behind more valuable things (like her sewing machine) than those sour-smelling, musty, clammy, bumpy featherbeds leaking their down all over our hair and clothes like dirty slush. Moreover, the sharp, rough stems of feathers (feathers from chickens dragging their sticky twisted wings behind them) showing through the thin threadbare cloth cover, their drab and lusterless reddish-black hue, made it clear that the down was as fraudulent as the featherbeds were uncomfortable: it contained only a minimum of plumage from force-fed Pannonian geese, the rest coming from disease-infected chicken coops. Mother was doubtless aware of the fraud, which made its way into both our dreams and our sleepless nights, but those moth-eaten featherbeds meant as much to her as the relics of my childhood—my father's papers and my books—meant to me. For her they were the symbol of our childhood and her love for us, the memory of those idyllic evening hours when she would fold them, still new in their cambric covers, under our backs and legs, puffing up the huge sour dough with her open hand and covering us so all that stuck out was our curly hair and the red tips of our noses. . .

I cannot believe that Mother failed to perceive the terrible fact I was unaware of at that time: that those featherbeds filled with would-be goose feathers were merely a continuation or, rather, the final chapter in the story of my father's Ahasuerus-like wanderings—which in fact began with his feather-merchant ancestors, arriving here from the distant murk of history—the heavy, hereditary burden we still dragged with us everywhere, pointlessly.

THE BOY AND THE DOG

A Talking Dog

I was born, as my mother tells it, of a light-hearted fling that brought her seven children and much misery. Two of my brothers and one sister died at birth. I first opened my eyes to the light of day early one autumn during the war in the house of Mrs. Albina Knipper, the village midwife. Both my mother and Mrs. Knipper took good care of me, fed and petted me. My basket was lined with rags and feathers like a bird's nest. My mother taught me what life is: how to wag my tail, how to show my fangs, how to clean the gum from my eyes, and how to chase pesky flies. We also practiced the basic forms of attack and defense. It was great fun and perfectly safe: we would jump at each other like village mutts, but we never used our fangs and kept our claws in our paws, like daggers in scabbards.

Then one day they took me from my mother, and that was the day my life as a dog began. (I know people say, "It's a dog's life" to mean a hard life, but I'm not complaining. All I mean is that my life began per se.)

When Mr. Berki (for that was the name of my future lord and master) paid Mrs. Knipper, he hadn't yet decided which of us would go with him and I understood little of what was going on around me. All I remember is that Mother was very unhappy and cried and cried. Not until much later did I realize why she failed to take the initiative and resist. It was for my own good, actually. Who knows what fate would have had in store for me if Mr. Berki hadn't taken me in. Of the four of us left at the time, only two are still alive. Me and my brother. He was sold to a hunter from another village. And here is what happened to my sisters: Mrs. Knipper tied a rock around their necks and threw them into the raging river. Not that she liked doing it. I know she'd have taken pity on them if there hadn't been a war on. For my mother's sake at least. Because Mrs. Knipper loved animals—even nasty cats—but what do you expect. As that great animal lover La Fontaine would have said, *"A la guerre comme à la guerre."* All's fair in love and war.

My mother went out of her mind with grief. She wouldn't eat for days; she cried and moaned, racing around the yard and the village, peering into every nook and cranny. Then one day Mrs. Knipper said to her, "Lola," she said (because that was my mother's name), "I had to! Forgive me, Lola. I just had to."

My mother happened to be lying next to her at the time and, pricking up her ears to catch Mrs. Knipper's every word, she gazed over at her so sadly, her eyes brimming with tears, that Mrs. Knipper burst into tears herself and said, "Please, Lola, Please! Don't look at me like that! I had to do it. You know what hard times we're going through."

But my mother, mad with grief, kept looking her straight in the eye.

"Please, Lola, please! Don't look at me like that," said Mrs. Knipper. "I threw them in the river."

Realizing her worst fears were true, my mother let out a howl and made for the river. She raced downstream, whimpering like a dog or, God forgive me, a human. She found my sisters grounded on a sandbank in a patch of reeds near the next village. The rock was still around their necks.

She came home that evening only to die at my side.

✲

One day, lying on the veranda of Mr. Berki, my new owner, pondering my fate—thinking about my poor mother, my brothers and sisters, Mrs. Knipper, and life in general—I began to whimper, more with grief than cold.

And all at once a boy appeared and started petting me and warming me with his hands as if I were, God forbid, more sparrow than dog. He looked me in the face and laughed and called out, "Anna! Anna! Come and see! A sparrow!"

"Oh, how sweet!" said Anna and pinched my cheek.

"This dog reminds me of somebody," said the boy. "Really he does."

"You're right," said Anna. "Who can it be?"

"You mean you think so too!"

"I could die laughing," his sister said.

"So could I," said the boy. He had cupped his hands and was holding me in them like a sparrow.

"I know who," said the boy's sister.

"Tell me, Anna. Who? Please! Tell me. Who is it?"

"Who do you think?" said Anna. "Guess."

"No, tell me," said the boy. "I can't. I only know he really. . . I could die laughing too!"

"Here's a hint," said Anna. "It's an old woman."

"Mrs. Knipper!" the boy cried. "The midwife!"

"I could die laughing," his sister said. "The spitting image!"

❋

So I began to wonder whether I looked like Mrs. Knipper, though I must say I'd never seen the resemblance before. Maybe our grief gave us similar expressions: Mrs. Knipper was terribly unhappy about what she'd done and I missed my family. If you want to know who I really looked like, it was my mother. I had her dark eyes— deep purple, like plums—and her ears. The only thing I may have inherited from my father (I never knew him) was my build, because I later developed into a rather slim dog with long legs, which, if I remember correctly, my mother did not have. From my mother I also inherited the color of my coat—brownish-red—and most of my character traits: sensitivity, humility, patience, fidelity, devotion, excitability, as well as a certain lazy, light-hearted attitude.

A dog like me has no thrilling story to tell. I had a fairly happy childhood (except for the forced break-up of my family, of course) even though it coincided with the war. Or maybe because it did. Let me explain. War tears people apart; they lose their humanity. War teaches people fear; it makes them suspicious. A dog like me—a faithful, devoted pet—means a lot in such conditions. If you're not a child and you're not supersensitive, you can love a dog without worry, without fear you'll go mad or die of grief if the war takes him from you; you can love him wholeheartedly, you can tell him your every thought without fear he will betray your secrets and hidden desires. In times of war a dog has trouble surviving only until his fangs grow in. (My sisters—may they rest in peace—perished for want of them.) But for a grown-up dog, a good strong dog, war is bliss. There are always livestock epidemics and horses falling in battle, and the soldiers barely bury them. Just so dogs and Gypsies won't get them, as they say.

Who cares about my biography anyway? I am not a famous hunter (or even a decent one) or known for my speed, and I not only lack noble blood and a pedigree, I was to all intents and purposes born out of wedlock and am thus illegitimate, a bastard. Nor have I distinguished myself on the battlefield and had a monument erected in my honor or been decorated by the Red Cross—or anyone else for that matter. In other words, I'm just an ordinary dog, and my lot is nothing special. The only thing that lifts me out of the ordinary is my power of speech. And the reason I was granted it was my love for that boy. My unhappy love, I might say.

❄

One morning my new master Mr. Berki came in with a young boy and said to him, "What do you think of this dog, Andy?"

"I think he's super!" the boy said. (He liked to exaggerate.) "What are you going to call him?"

"Dingo," said Mr. Berki.

"Dingo?" said the boy. "I don't like it. What does it mean?"

"A dingo is a wild Australian dog," said Mr. Berki.

"Then I do like it," said the boy. "Very much."

Even though Mr. Berki was my official master, I belonged body and soul to the boy. I got on better with him

than with anyone else in the world. We understood each
other. It helped a lot that he was young but also that we
shared certain traits. In fact, I don't think it would be
going too far to say that we had a lot in common: we
were both lazy, undisciplined, and loyal, and we both
loved adventure. I can also say that the boy had something of the dog in him: his sense of smell, for example,
his sensitivity to scents—I'm sure I'm right. We were
also linked by our loneliness and longings. His longing
for his father and mine for my family—they created a
kind of bond between us. When I suddenly began to
grow and gain the respect of the village mutts as the wise
and learned dog of a wise young master, the boy grew
less solitary, more adventuresome. Because I did more
than rid him of his inborn fear of dogs (which his father
had too); I made him braver in general: he knew he had
a dependable, faithful protector in me. In exchange, he
taught me various useful skills that increased my reputa-
tion. Thanks to him I was able to round up stray cows,
dig up molehills (which we did for fun, to pass the time),
chase rabbits, sniff out fox dens and the nests of swamp
fowl, and catch wild ducks, frogs, butterflies, snakes. I
even learned how to talk to him in his hours of solitude!
I remember the day we lost a cow named Orange and almost ran away together. He gave me difficult, responsi-
ble things to do that day, one of which made me feel
more like a carrier pigeon than a dog. We often planned
to run away—whenever we were unhappy—but we
never got farther than the third village. Sometimes the

boy told or read me stories. I don't believe it's an exaggeration to say I know the novel *Man, Horse, Dog* by heart: he told it to the shepherds many times, often making up parts of his own.

No, my life is no novel; it's more like a book of short stories, many short adventures, happy and sad, but the boy is present in every one of them just as I am present in his.

I've noticed the boy has been sad lately. He's been a little colder, a little more distant to me as well. I can tell he's hiding something from me. But I've finally got to the bottom of it, and my old canine melancholy is back. The boy is planning to run away again, but this time for real! There can be no doubt. I know why he's avoiding me: he wants to make the separation easier. And I'm so low I feel ill. I lie dozing at the front door to make sure he can't leave without saying good-bye. I just lie there dozing and thinking through my life.

I don't think I'll survive the separation.

A-ooo! A-ooo!

A Letter

Dear Mr. Berki,

I am writing from far away to say hello. I hope you are well. I am slowly making friends in school, even though they make fun of my accent. I still dream of being back home with you, and just last night Mama woke me be-

cause I was crying in my sleep. Mama says it's homesick-
ness and will soon pass.

Please don't laugh at me for what I'm going to say
now, Mr. Berki, but the main reason I cried last night
was my dog Dingo. Anna keeps making fun of me. She
says I'm in love with that dog, and maybe she's right, but
I'm sure you'll understand and won't laugh at me.

What I want to tell you about is how hard it was for
me the day we left and I had to say good-bye. Remember
how I disappeared just before the cart was supposed to
go and I didn't come back until the last minute and
everybody bawled me out? Well, let me tell you where I
was. I was down at the river saying good-bye to Dingo.
Then I tied him to a willow and he didn't put up a strug-
gle, he just whimpered. True, he wanted to follow me
and begged me to undo him, but I told him to stay. I told
him that was life and I knew I'd never have a better
friend, a better dog-friend or people-friend. And then I
heard them calling me and I ran home to say good-bye to
all of you. Remember? We all cried—my mother and
Anna and your mother and you. We knew we'd never
see one another again. Then the cart started off and I
cried so hard I thought my heart would burst. I thought
of all the years we'd spent with you, I thought of my poor
dead father who never returned, of you and your
mother, of Mrs. Rigó my teacher, of Béla Hermann and
Laci Tóth and Júlia Szabó and all the rest. I didn't dare
turn around because it would have made me cry even
harder to see the village and the steeple and the Count's

Woods and everything one last time. But I couldn't stop myself. And you know what I saw, Mr. Berki? I saw Dingo running after us, whimpering, whimpering as loud as he could! And I asked old man Martin to chase him away with his whip and to make the horses go faster, because I couldn't stand it. Dingo was ready to drop, you can be sure. He'd followed us all the way to Csesztreg! His muzzle was all foamy and his tongue was hanging out. I started screaming and yelling, and old man Martin had to give him a good whipping before he got him to stop or rather collapse in the middle of the road. Even when we were in the train I kept looking out of the window and crying. I kept thinking I could hear him whimper and he was still running after us.

That's all I wanted to tell you, Mr. Berki. But I wanted to ask you to write back about everything and tell me how Dingo is doing. I also wanted to ask you—if you don't think I'm being too silly—to read my letter out loud to him and tell him it isn't my fault I couldn't take him with me and I'll never forget him. Tell him that one day when I'm a poet I'm going to write a poem or a fable about him. And in that fable the dog will have the power of speech. And his name will be Dingo, of course. Please do what I ask, Mr. Berki. He'll understand. All you have to do is look him in the eye when you talk and keep saying my name. Tell him "Andy, Andy, Andy says hello." Speak to him slowly, the way you would to a child. He'll understand. You'll see. He'll start to whimper the moment you mention my name. And that will mean he understands.

One last thing. Please look after him and buy him a good dinner with the money I am enclosing. What he likes best of all is horse meat (with lots of bones). I'm sure you can find some in Baksa at the butcher's. Mr. Fejes. Please don't mention the money in your letter to Mama (it comes from my savings) because Anna would make fun of me. The best thing would be for you to write to me personally.

Well, that's all for now. Please give my best wishes to your mother and Mrs. Rigó, to all my friends, especially Béla Hermann, Laci Tóth, and Júlia Szabó and tell them I think of them often.

Your poor friend,
Andreas Sam, Schoolchild

The Response

Dear Andy,

I am glad to hear you are well and making progress in school, as I can tell from your mother's letter, and, as I can tell from your letter, that you are still good at composition and your penmanship is improving. I believe you will one day be a poet, and if your deceased father is any indication you will not want for imagination.

As for your request, my dear poet, all I can say is that

I would have been only too glad to carry it out if it hadn't been for a turn of events that you will be very sad to hear about.

The day you left, Dingo came home tired and battered, whimpering and howling. He wouldn't eat a thing all day, though we even offered him liver. He just drank water, drank and drank.

The next day we found him at the front door, dead.

Dear Andy, try not to be too sad. There are worse things in life—you'll see when you grow up. All I can say is that I was very sorry too. He was truly a fine dog. My mother even cried. But you'll get over it; you'll even forget it all some day.

I am enclosing your money (plus interest). Use it to buy a fountain pen. Then try and write a composition about what happened, in verse or in prose, and send it to me. If it's good, I'll show it to Mrs. Rigó, your teacher. It will certainly make her happy. If she likes it, she may even have it published in *The Good Pastor.*

All your friends send their greetings.

Be good and try not to be too sad.

Your friend,
Mr. Berki

THE AEOLIAN HARP

The harp is an instrument that more than any other illustrates the medieval formula of combining the beautiful (*perfectio prima*) with the useful (*perfectio secunda*), pleasing the eye, which means satisfying the rules of formal harmony, but above all fulfilling its basic purpose: to make a pleasant sound.

I had a harp when I was nine. It consisted of a telegraph pole and six pairs of electric wires connected to six porcelain insulators that looked like an incomplete tea service (incomplete, because I had damaged one of them with my slingshot before discovering the Chinese porcelain's musical function).

Now that I have described the basic components of the instrument, let me proceed to the particulars.

Making an aeolian harp calls for the porcelain buttons mentioned above to tune the strings and at least two poles—two telegraph poles made of plain tarred fir—to hold them up. The ideal distance between the poles is fifty meters. The poles need to be exposed to the successive influence of rain, frost, and sun for a minimum of five to ten years so that abrupt changes in temperature (from +36°C to −22°C) can split the wood along its length. And it splits like a broken heart when it realizes it has ceased once and for all to be a tree, a young fir, and has become once and for all a telegraph pole.

When the wounded, split tree realizes it has been driven into the ground up to its knees and farther and has no chance of escape, there is nothing for it to do but gaze into the distance at the woods, which nod back.

And to accept the fact that its closest friends, friends and comrades, are the two poles fifty meters to the left and to the right, they too equally disheartened and driven into the ground up to their knees.

Now when the poles are connected by wires and topped not by green branches but by a Chinese tea set (six cups turned upside down and thus unfit to drink from, even for birds), they begin to sing and pluck their strings. All you have to do is put your ear up to the pole. Though it is no longer a pole; it is a harp.

Inexperienced readers (who have never put their ears to a telegraph pole) may think it also requires wind. Not at all. The ideal time for my harp is a hot day in July, one of the dog days, when the air quivers so with heat you see mirages, when the wood is so dry and resonant it sounds hollow.

I almost forgot: the ideal place for my harp is along an ancient road. The one I have in mind lined the old post road, which dates back to the times when Pannonia was being settled by the Romans. As a result, the harp's column, acting as an antenna, captures sounds from ancient times; indeed, melodies waft in from the future as well. One set of strings covers an entire octave and can modulate easily between the major and minor mode.

So much for the instrument itself.

Now all that is left to do is turn and make certain there is no one on the Royal Road, no one in the wheat fields, no one in the ditch, no one on the horizon. If a cart laden with hay, alfalfa, or rye should happen by, the thing to do is run and hide in the drainage ditch beneath the road and wait for it to pass.

You will have understood by now: you must be completely alone. Otherwise people will start going on about how you're as crazy as your father and wondering what you're doing with your ear against a telegraph pole. Then someone will think you are silly enough to believe that there are bees swarming in the dry, swollen telegraph pole and are after honey; someone else will say you are listening for the arrival of allied aircraft so you can report it to the authorities; and there are those who will let their imagination run away with them and claim you are receiving secret messages from the cosmos.

Which is why (among other reasons) you would do well to see there is no one on the Royal Road, no one in the wheat fields, no one in the ditch, no one on the horizon.

I must admit that if a person with no music put his ear to the telegraph pole he might in fact believe he was hearing the buzz of aircraft and therefore run and hide in the ditch or dash into the village to report a bomber squadron. But that is just the first (false) impression; it is only the accompaniment, the *basso ostinato* in which the boy perceives the sound of time, because the sounds waft in from the depths of time and history as if from quasars, from far-off stars. (The smell of melted tar is merely a stimulant like the scent of burning herbs, sandalwood, or incense in church.)

And here is what the harp sings into his ear while he listens with his eyes shut: that he will soon stop tending cows for Mr. Molnár, that his father will never return, that he will leave the hut with the earthen floor, that he will finally go to his grandfather's in Montenegro, that he will get new books, that he will have fifteen hundred pencils, two hundred fountain pens, and five thousand books, that his mother will soon die, that he will meet a girl he will love forever, that he will travel, that he will see oceans and cities, that he will go back into ancient history, biblical times, and investigate his murky past, and that he will write the story of the aeolian harp made of telegraph poles and electric wires.

Postscript: Although the story "The Aeolian Harp" was written about fifteen years after the appearance of Early Sorrows, *it is thematically related to the cycle. I have therefore incorporated it into the collection at the end of the ballad as a kind of lyrical epilogue.*

—*Danilo Kiš*

BIRTH
CERTIFICATE
(A SHORT
AUTOBIOGRAPHY)

My father came into the world in western Hungary and was educated at the school of commerce in the native city of a certain Mr. Virág, who, by the grace of Mr. Joyce, eventually became the famous Leopold Bloom. I believe it was the liberal policy of Franz Josef II together with a desire for integration that led my grandfather to Magyarize the surname of his underage son, though many details of the family chronicle will remain forever obscure: in 1944 my father and all our relatives were taken off to Auschwitz, and almost none returned.

Among my mother's ancestors is a legendary Montenegrin hero who learned to read and write at the age of fifty, thereby adding the glory of the pen to the glory of the sword, and an "Amazon" who took revenge on a Turkish despot by cutting off his head. The ethnographic rarity I represent will die out with me.

In 1939, when I was four and anti-Jewish laws were being promulgated in Hungary, my parents had me baptized in the Orthodox faith at the Church of the Assumption in Novi Sad. It saved my life. Until the age of thirteen, I lived in my father's native region in Hungary, to which we fled in 1942, following the Novi Sad massacre. I worked as a servant for rich peasants, and in school I went to catechism and Catholic Bible study. The "troubling strangeness" that Freud calls *Heimlichkeit* would be my basic literary and metaphysical stimulus. At the age of nine I wrote my first poems, in Hungarian; one was about hunger, the other was a love poem par excellence.

From my mother I inherited a propensity for telling tales with a mixture of fact and legend; from my father—pathos and irony. My relationship to literature has also been affected by the fact that my father was the author of an international timetable, an entire cosmopolitan and literary legacy in itself.

My mother was a reader of novels until the age of twenty, when she realized, not without regret, that they were "fabrications," and rejected them for good. Her aversion to "pure fabrication" is latent in me as well.

BIRTH CERTIFICATE (A SHORT AUTOBIOGRAPHY)

In 1947 we were repatriated by the Red Cross to Montenegro, the home of my uncle, a well-known historian and a biographer of and commentator on Njegoš.* Immediately after we arrived, I took the art-school entrance examination. The bust of Voltaire we were asked to draw—a plaster cast of Houdon's statue—reminded me of an elderly German woman I knew in Novi Sad, and that is how I drew him. I was accepted nonetheless, probably on the basis of other work. I had to wait a year or two until I had the necessary academic preparation. During that time I decided to complete the Gymnasium program instead.

For two years I studied violin at the local music school, where I was taught by Simonuti Senior, whom we called "Paganini" not only for his appearance but for his love of vibrato. Just as I reached the second position, the music school moved to Kotor. I went on playing by ear, specializing in Gypsy music, Hungarian romances, and—at school dances—the tango and "English" waltzes.

At the Gymnasium I continued to write poetry. I also translated Hungarian, Russian, and French poets, primarily as a stylistic and linguistic exercise: I was training to be a poet, learning the craft of literature. We were taught Russian by White Army officers, émigrés from

---

* Petar Petrović Njegoš (1813–51), Prince-Bishop of Montenegro and author of *The Mountain Wreath,* a long philosophical poem considered one of the masterworks of Serb literature.

the twenties who substituted for absent teachers and were equally at home in mathematics, physics, chemistry, French, and Latin.

From the Gymnasium I entered the University of Belgrade, where I was the first student to graduate from the newly created Department of Comparative Literature.

As an instructor in Serbo-Croatian language and literature I have taught at Strasbourg, Bordeaux, and Lille: for the last few years I have been living in Paris, in the tenth arrondissement, and am not at all homesick. At times I wake up not knowing where I am; I hear my compatriots calling to one another and an accordion blaring from a cassette player in a car parked beneath my window.

1983

Danilo Kiš died in Paris of lung cancer in 1989.